What people are saying about …

RELENTLESS PURSUIT

"I've read many books about how to start a business, a ministry, or an idea. But in *Relentless Pursuit*, Ben provides the tools, experiences, and wisdom to help break through the difficult times on your journey. As you learn from the stories of several incredible leaders, this book will give you the spark of inspiration you need to pursue your dream and never give up."

—**Craig Groeschel**, founding and
senior pastor of Life.Church; host of the
Craig Groeschel Leadership Podcast

"One thing I love to ask leaders is, 'What advice would you give to the younger generation?' I find hindsight from experienced men and women to be one of the most valuable forms of teaching I can receive. This book is filled with the answer to that question from incredible leaders who have walked the road, made the mistakes, and now can offer their advice to those who come after them. You would be wise to absorb the wisdom contained in these pages and apply it to your leadership and life journey."

—**Banning Liebscher**, founder
and pastor of Jesus Culture

"Ben's skill is not just teaching others how to lead, but also bringing leaders alongside him that we can teach from a variety of experiences.

Relentless Pursuit is required reading for anyone who is thinking of starting a venture, anyone who is struggling to maintain momentum, and anyone who wants to see the vision they have become a reality. I can't recommend this book highly enough."

—**Dr. Robi Sonderegger**, clinical psychologist; founder of Psychology Cafe

"In order to bring change, courageous leadership is required. Ben Cooley is such a leader and the pages of this book will ignite passion and awaken purpose. We can all make a difference but must first decide what we will relentlessly pursue."

—**Charlotte Gambill**, author; speaker; lead pastor of LIFE Church, UK

"For many years I have admired the passion, drive, and excellence that Hope for Justice has applied in the fight against human trafficking. Ben Cooley is a visionary leader who has an incredible gifting to not only start an organization but build a movement."

—**Sir Brian Souter**, founder and chairman of Stagecoach Group

"I have known Ben Cooley a long time. He models a different kind of leadership, one that is innovative, humble, and mostly importantly effective. In this book, he manages to communicate how we could all lead differently and make a real difference in the world. We at Rend Collective love Ben Cooley!"

—**Gareth Gilkeson**, Rend Collective

RELENTLESS PURSUIT

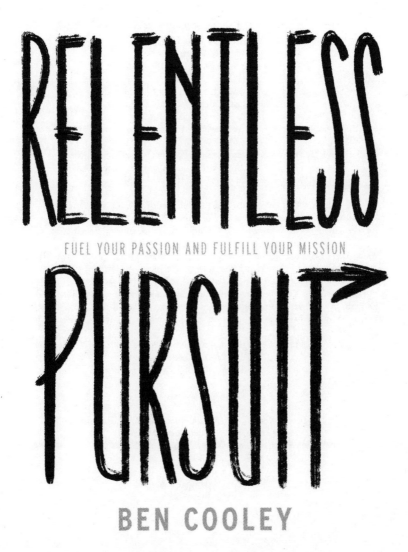

RELENTLESS

FUEL YOUR PASSION AND FULFILL YOUR MISSION

PURSUIT

BEN COOLEY

DAVID C COOK

transforming lives together

RELENTLESS PURSUIT
Published by David C Cook
4050 Lee Vance Drive
Colorado Springs, CO 80918 U.S.A.

Integrity Music Limited, a Division of David C Cook
Brighton, East Sussex BN1 2RE, England

The graphic circle C logo is a registered trademark of David C Cook.

The website addresses recommended throughout this book are offered as a
resource to you. These websites are not intended in any way to be or imply an
endorsement on the part of David C Cook, nor do we vouch for their content.

Unless otherwise noted, all Scripture quotations are taken from THE HOLY BIBLE,
NEW INTERNATIONAL VERSION®, NIV® Copyright © 1973, 1978, 1984,
2011 by Biblica, Inc.® Used by permission. All rights reserved worldwide. Scripture
quotations marked KJV are taken from the King James Version of the Bible. (Public
Domain.); NASB are taken from the New American Standard Bible®, copyright ©
1960, 1995 by The Lockman Foundation. Used by permission. (www.Lockman.org).

Library of Congress Control Number 2019940997
ISBN 978-0-8307-7850-8
eISBN 978-0-8307-7857-7

The Team: Wendi Lord, Alice Crider, Jeff Gerke, Rachael
Stevenson, Jon Middel, Susan Murdock
Cover Design: Nick Lee
Cover Photo: Getty Images

Printed in the United Kingdom
First Edition 2019

1 2 3 4 5 6 7 8 9 10

070819

Dedicated to Deb, Isabel, and Lilly. This journey would not have been possible without you.

To all at Team Hope for Justice, you all inspire me. Gareth and Josh, you have been outstanding in your support.

And to all the wonderful, brilliant team at David C Cook, I am humbled by your belief.

CONTENTS

FOREWORD

Leadership is not about a performance or a platform; it is about people. As lead pastor at !Audacious Church in England, I interact with people from all types of backgrounds. The trajectory of life can be so different for so many people, but the one thing that unites us all is that we each have a purpose.

The question is whether we pursue that purpose or reject it.

What you do with your life matters! Not just to you but also to those around you.

The name of our church means "to be bold, daring, dangerous, fearless, unrestrained by convention, and to challenge assumptions." If there is anyone who embodies the name "Audacious," it is Ben and Deb Cooley.

Anyone who starts an organization at the age of twenty-six, books an arena, attracts almost six thousand people, and then over ten years builds a global network rescuing and restoring victims of human trafficking is someone unrestrained by convention.

Vision is vital. It is a clear image of a preferable future, and if you can "see it," you are halfway to getting it. Our vision at !Audacious

Church is that we build a church that stops traffic. When the main football (soccer) teams of our city play in Manchester, they cause traffic jams. We want this to be the case with the church.

One wise man wrote, "Where there is no vision, the people perish" (Prov. 29:18 KJV). Ben has a vision to see the end of modern slavery, and without such a vision, people will continue to be enslaved in the evil trade of human trafficking.

The key to vision is staying focused on why we do what we do. Businesses and churches alike fail when they forget their purpose. I'm not talking about a grand vision statement. I'm talking about something clear enough for people to visualize and put their energies behind.

Once you have that vision—and a tribe around you crazy enough to believe it—then with shared values, principles, and culture, anything is possible.

This book comes at a significant time for me, and I am sure it will for you too. It will encourage you to take your vision and thrive, even in the face of insurmountable obstacles.

I've known Ben for nearly ten years. We've spent a lot of time together through those years, and there are several things you need to know about him. He is authentic, passionate, crazy, disciplined, unrelenting, hilarious, humble, has no idea about football, and did I say *audacious*?

In *Relentless Pursuit* he has brought together leaders from business, music, charity, and church, and they have all been transparent about how they have relentlessly pursued their vision. If you read this book, you will not only be motivated to keep going but also gain a sense of relief that you are not the only one experiencing what you are going through right now. Others have experienced it too—and survived!

Vision shows us the preferable future. That future can become a reality only when we commit to a relentless pursuit.

Glyn Barrett
Senior Leader, !Audacious Church, UK

OUR WORDS FRAME OUR CULTURE

A few years ago, a pastor and longtime friend of mine invited me to speak at his large, growing church in South America. The church reaches thousands of people every week. The night before I was scheduled to speak, I talked to my friend about Hope for Justice and what we do to fight modern slavery. I described the extent of the issue in Southeast Asia, Europe, and North America. My friend was visibly disgusted as I told him that human beings were being bought and sold, treated as commodities.

Tears streamed from his eyes as I recalled story after story of lives that had been traded and exploited through modern slavery. As we sat in a restaurant near his church, he said to me, "Ben, this can't be happening in my city."

I was absolutely dumbfounded. Largely because my experience had led me to know that South America is one of the worst areas of human trafficking in the world. In fact, US State Department documents show that tens of thousands, if not hundreds of thousands, of children are exploited across South America every year.[1]

I said to him, "You know it *is* happening here, don't you?" He shook his head. I asked him whether he knew a taxi driver who could come collect us from the restaurant. He did, and when the taxi arrived, we got in and asked the driver to take us to the nearest brothel.

The taxi driver replied, "There are ten within two kilometers of this restaurant. Which one do you want to go to?"

Appalled, my pastor friend asked that he drive us to the nearest one.

I wouldn't normally go on a brothel investigation alone. That is not how our operations run. Normally we follow a process in which people with senior law enforcement experience, like former National Crime Agency and FBI employees, go in. We don't do things in a maverick or rogue way. But I believed this was a moment when God allowed me to see something and show this pastor something he needed to see.

The driver took us to a brothel unlike any I had seen on previous investigative trips. He didn't just drive to a brothel; he drove into a compound. Steel gates closed behind us. Lights cast a dim red glow across the site. There was a sense of people hiding in the shadows.

The pastor stayed in the taxi, but the driver opened my door, and I got out. I left the car, walked into the nearby building, then down the corridor and into a waiting area.

I couldn't believe what I saw in front of me. Girls as young as thirteen years old—there must have been as many as fifty of them sitting around the room—full of fear.

As I walked in, their eyes looked down in unison as if to say, "Please don't pick me."

When the madam walked in after me, the atmosphere changed and the girls started walking toward me. I didn't speak the language, so I made my excuses and left.

I walked back down the corridor, passed two security guards, then got back into the taxi. The engine started, and we drove out through the steel gates of the compound.

I can't describe the look on the pastor's face when I described what I'd seen. He was heartbroken and grieving. His sense of responsibility for his community rose up, and he wanted to do something to help these victims.

We drove to three brothels that night—all very similar in size and all guarded by large, intimidating men with guns.

All of them full of young, vulnerable girls.

The pastor asked the taxi driver question after question. What was going on? How extensive was the issue?

At one point the pastor gasped, and I asked what the driver had said.

"Ben," my friend said, "I was shocked that the girls were as young as you described. I was shocked that this was happening in my city. But the taxi driver has just informed me that the people who own this brothel specialize in serving police officers." We rode in silence after that. The information wasn't surprising to me, but I felt the outrage anew as I sat beside my friend.

I wrote this book because I firmly believe in good, ethical, and moral leadership. I believe that sort of leadership is needed in every sector of society to bring about lasting social change. How sorely we need it. It is not OK that leaders within our communities, like the police officers in that South American city, are contributors to injustice and abuse, especially of children.

If you are a leader, you must lead with the authority of integrity and justice.

Whether you are in business or in government, whether you're a stay-at-home parent or a teacher, whether you are a politician or a church leader, I believe you have a part to play in bringing about fairness, equality, justice, and moral leadership. I believe it is up to all kinds of leaders to change the tide and bring about the social change this world so desperately needs.

You might help bring about legislation to protect the poor and the marginalized. You might go into business so you can be an ethical employer who brings about social good. You could go into finance so you can affect the economy and bring about fairness and equality on a global scale.

Whatever you choose to do, I firmly believe that good leadership—good, ethical leadership—can change the world.

But the journey is not an easy one—every leadership journey provides challenges, every leadership journey requires stamina, and every leadership journey needs a tribe to support the vision.

This book will provide some of those tools to help you not only start something but also see your vision become a reality.

EVALUATED EXPERIENCE

You may be wondering, *Who is this Ben Cooley person? And how is it that he is the author of a book of stories from so many other people?* A bit of explanation is in order.

This book came out of a vision I had that stemmed from a conversation with a friend named Mick. Mick is a former deputy director of the Serious Organised Crime Agency (now the National Crime Agency) in the UK, which is a large national law enforcement agency that employs over five thousand specialist officers.

I was talking to Mick one day about my frustration with one employee from a law enforcement background. I was especially exasperated because I kept hearing the same statement: "I have thirty years' experience." Of course, that sounded really good to me. Thirty years' experience? That's fantastic! I didn't mind the comment. What frustrated me was that, time after time, it turned out all those years of experience didn't equate to much. Let's just say his performance wasn't at the level I'd been hoping.

Mick laughed, much to my surprise. "Ben," he said, "he probably doesn't have thirty years of experience as you understand it. He might have only one year specialist experience that he's simply continued to use for thirty years!"

I learned that experience is good, but *evaluated experience* is better. That's one lesson in this book.

I've been on the Hope for Justice journey for more than a decade. We now have hundreds of people on staff, offices around the world, and many high-ranking people on board who have much more experience than I do working with modern slavery and law enforcement. I wish I had known a few things when I'd started out, back when I was twenty-six years old. I wish I'd been stronger when I was starting out.

I don't have thirty years' experience, but I have more than ten years of *evaluated* experience. And that made me want to create a book that consolidated all the lessons I've learned so people could have them right out of the gate. I wanted a book that captures the highs, the lows, the disappointments, the frustrations, and the innovations that come when trying to do something that really matters in the world. I wanted a book that would take all that and weave it together in a letter to my twenty-six-year-old self. I wanted it to be just for me, you know? Just for dear, twenty-six-year-old me.

But then I realized that all leaders wish they knew then what they know now. So many successful people—billionaires, musicians, business leaders, and nonprofit CEOs—have said, "Ben, I wish I'd known this when I started out!"

That's what caused me to create the podcast series called *Dear 26 Year Old Me*. In it I interview leaders and ask them what they wish they'd known when they were just getting going. And now you're reading a book that's an outgrowth of that series.

It is our responsibility as leaders to pass on our knowledge and set up the next generation to win. My lesson of pain is not just a lesson *I* need to learn. But that evaluated experience can be passed on to the next generation.

Relentless Pursuit is a consolidated learning from highly successful people who have done big things and stayed the course when circumstances looked impossible. They aren't just the pinnacle of all leaders. They aren't just people who made lots of money. They've made plenty of mistakes as well. But after all they've learned along the way, they agreed to produce this resource so you can be a healthier, more effective leader.

For today and not just years down the line.

A WORD ON FAITH

Whether or not you are a person of faith, I'm glad you're reading this book. My hope is that you will be challenged and encouraged by the advice and experience of the contributors, some of whom share my faith. But whether you are Christian, Buddhist, Muslim, or agnostic, I hope that after reading this book, you are inspired to not only conceive a vision but also see that vision through to becoming a reality. May you relentlessly pursue your passion and mission!

THE JOY OF THE MIDDLE

Good leaders are always expanding their capabilities. I expect you already know how you want to grow and develop. Perhaps it's to make your ministry or your organization bigger, smarter, more equipped, more impactful, or more successful. And you may be looking to develop not only in business and work but also in your families and key relationships.

There is so much we want to achieve with our lives. But the journey isn't the same in all seasons and phases. There is one set of activities and skills you need at the outset of your endeavor, other sets you need to develop along the way, and yet another set you need in order to end or hand things off well.

Many times—be it in business, marriages, families, ministries, or campaigns to change the world—it's possible to begin well and have incredible momentum at first, even getting far beyond where you thought you'd be, and then to encounter challenges and obstacles that slow you down and perhaps even block the way. The skills needed to get going may not work as well when it comes to the effort to keep going.

We need to learn how to press on through the glorious middle stretch, when the initial euphoria wears off and it "gets real" and becomes a genuine struggle, sometimes against entrenched opposition. Yet the people whom I have seen succeed at their big, God-sized objectives are those who found a way to maintain momentum, especially in those times. Everyone can start, but it is those who relentlessly pursue their dreams, their *impossibles*, who see those dreams become reality. It's those who have endurance in the middle who win through to the end.

Years ago, I took part in a bicycle challenge to raise money. In Zoe's Challenge we cycled the route that was traveled by one of the first girls Hope for Justice rescued from modern slavery. Zoe (not her real name) was trafficked from Latvia to Southampton, England, so we retraced the route as a fund-raising challenge to rescue more children from slavery. With the help of a ferry to cross the English Channel, we cycled all the way from Latvia (which borders Russia) to Southampton.

I say it was a challenge, and it was, not only because of the distance but also because I hate cycling! Let's just think about this for a moment: I was wearing spandex … every day … for nineteen days … across 2,715 kilometers (1,687 miles). I just want you to know it was not an enjoyable experience. That's more miles than the Tour de France—done in fewer days!

In a multiday endurance race like that, where do you think the biggest challenge was? At what stage in the race do you think most riders dropped out?

The challenge was not at the start, way up in Latvia. Starting out, we were all rested and ready for the journey ahead. The challenge wasn't at the beginning, because I was about to embark on the pursuit of my vision. The challenge wasn't at the end either, 2,715 kilometers away in Southampton. The challenge wasn't near the end, because when I was so close to it, I could see the finish line.

The challenge is always in the middle.

The hard part of marriage is not right at the start, because you are so in love! The challenge comes when familiarity breeds contempt and when tiredness, stress, children, and financial strain come in. In the middle is when it gets difficult. Somehow you need to keep pursuing, to find the momentum to keep pushing through.

In year one of your business, you are so excited. But it's in years two and three that the challenges hit. People leave. The objectives prove difficult to reach. Competition increases. Key alliances fail. Your team begins to lose the vision.

When you start a church, there is often huge momentum. But around year three or year four, people sometimes look for something new.

Here you will find the endurance to push through to the successful realization of your vision. I want to see you complete the race so that what once seemed impossible (at least to others) becomes reality.

HOW I STARTED

I started an organization at the age of twenty-six after hearing about modern-day slavery one night in Manchester, England. I walked out of a building and thought, *If that was my daughter, I would do something about it.*

It was the next thought that transformed the course of my life: *She is* someone's *daughter. I* should *do something about it.*

So I booked the NEC Arena in Birmingham, England. We saw 5,884 people attend our first event, and we shared with them about modern slavery and how they could help.

From there, over the last ten-plus years, the movement has spread into nine countries and twenty-three locations. Over the last eleven months, as I have been writing this book, we reached over sixty-three thousand children. More than four thousand children went through our outreach programs. We now have hundreds of staff members. We are expanding fast, and we are expanding globally.

In fact, in the last year we have had record numbers of people helped. Not only have we expanded the charity, but we have also launched a business called Slave-Free Alliance, helping businesses address slavery in their supply chains. We now serve some of the largest businesses in the world, addressing human rights issues, protecting their supply chains, and helping them move toward slave-free products and services.

I actually love my job. It's not easy, but I love it! The other day I was in Uganda with one of the girls we have helped in our Lighthouse program. (That is our short-term residential program for victims of modern slavery. It's a trauma-informed program to help victims become whole again. We call it Lighthouse because we want to lead them safely to harbor.) Thecla (not her real name) ran away from home, hoping to meet friends in the big city of Kampala, but she couldn't find them. That's where her nightmare began.

Thecla was exploited by men in the most graphic and horrendous way. It never ceases to shock me what a fellow human being can do to an innocent child. Thankfully our team was able to help her, and she was referred to our Lighthouse program. After some time she started to feel able to move past what had happened to her and started to feel whole again. After months of counseling and care, we were able to do one of my favorite things we do at Hope for Justice: we took her *home*!

Oh, my friend, I wish you could have heard the screams of joy when her family greeted her. The tears that streamed down her face, the long-extended hugs, her father's pure joy at having his baby girl back *home*. In a world with so much bad news, this day was a win.

WORDS CREATE THINGS

If you look at the first page in the Bible, you'll see that it says, "In the beginning God created the heavens and the earth." Just a bit later on, it says, "God said, 'Let there be light,' and there was light" (Gen. 1:1, 3). Let's look at that for a moment.

God spoke. But His speaking couldn't have been for the purpose of communication—because no one was there to hear. When God first used His words, it was not for communication but for creation.

Throughout history, when people have used words for more than communication, they have created something. When Dr. Martin Luther King Jr. said "I have a dream," his words created something. When William Wilberforce spoke out against slavery in the British Parliament, his words created.

The same goes for us and our words. They have the power to do more than communicate. They have the power to create—for good or ill.

I'll never forget when a teacher told me, "Ben, you'll never be able to achieve anything." Can you imagine the impact those words had on me as a young person? Here was a teacher with what I assumed was a superior vantage point about life, assessing me as a person and declaring that I would never achieve anything worthwhile! For years I wore that badge. For years I accepted those words as true. They created, all right. They created a negative, crushing portrait of me that I believed. Until the day when I could finally see the lie of it and throw it off. But the point remains: our words can absolutely amplify the good in people … or they can absolutely destroy people.

This is why, at Hope for Justice, we are extremely deliberate with our language. If there is one thing I will pull my team up on, it is their language. We should always speak life. When others criticize us, we have determined to be life giving to them. We want to be the organization that always speaks life about others. Words frame our culture, so we have decided to use our words as God does: to create some good stuff.

The world gives us enough words meant to destroy us, doesn't it? Do we need to contribute to those? Many of us have been in environments where those we trusted have spoken negative messages to us: "You can't …" "You will never …" "Why are you such a …?" Those words lodge in our souls, and we repeat them to ourselves like a mantra over our lives.

I can't … I will never … Why am I such a …?

And we live with those messages as if they were true, because someone we thought saw us clearly spoke them over our lives.

Words are powerful things. The power of life and death is in the tongue (see Prov. 18:21). If this is true, then it means you as a leader have an incredible power with your words to create the sort of team and environment you want. You have the power to change the thinking of yourself and your team.

That should invigorate you. With something as simple as words spoken from your mouth, you can give life and create a place where hope and joy reign.

What I am trying to do starts with the power to pursue the impossible, which is a vision created through our words. We are all able to speak positively over our lives. We use our words not by accident but deliberately and with intention.

Some of my friends have been in a position to build their own houses. I have never met a person who has built his or her house by accident. If you are going to build a house, you employ an architect first, then a builder.

An architect creates the plan. That's exactly what your words need to do: create the plan of who you are going to be and what you are going to achieve.

I want this book to help you, to shape you, and to create something good in you. Let's go on this journey together and pursue our impossible.

DO NOT STAND STILL

Relentless Pursuit is composed of personal accounts of perseverance from some of the most successful people I know or have ever heard of. I am privileged to call them my friends. Some have started local churches. Others have started multibillion-dollar businesses. Some have been successful in the music industry. Some are in ministry. These are the sort of people you hope to become someday.

Wouldn't you know it? They've all been where you are. They've all begun great endeavors with the loftiest goals, or else they've been enabled to pursue lofty goals because of the success of their endeavors. And they've all run into obstacles and challenges in that glorious middle phase that might've caused them to abandon their efforts. They all pressed on to success, and now you can hear their stories and their advice.

Momentum needs movement. My hope is that you will be inspired to make the moves that will increase your momentum.

Each chapter features a different contributor sharing his or her story and wisdom. At the end of each chapter, you'll encounter questions I really want you to wrestle with. I don't want you to just scan the questions and think, *Yeah, no, I'm on to the next chapter!* Because if you are like me, you might want to read this and just look for the sound bites.

No. This isn't that book.

This book has been written for you to pause. To ask yourself questions. To ask questions of those around you.

In my interviews with these highly successful people, I have attempted to ask the best questions. I am a firm believer in the idea that the best leaders ask the best questions. Some questions you wish had been asked will be missing. Some questions will be appropriate only to your context. Write down those questions. Then write down what is going to change as a result of being challenged by that chapter. That's the whole point, really. Without action—without movement—there is no momentum and no pursuit of your impossible.

Do not stand still.

Do not do what you have always done. If you did that, you already know you would get what you have always got. This book is designed to create a *shift* in who you are so you can take new actions and get new results.

We are going to get there, my friend; we are going to reach that goal. We may have difficult days ahead, because change and movement are difficult. But they are also vital in sustaining momentum.

DISCUSSION QUESTIONS

1. What's a concern you became aware of that caused you to go from thinking *Someone should do something about this* to *I have to do something about this*?
2. What's the most powerfully *negative* thing someone ever said about you? What's the most powerfully *positive* thing someone has said about you?
3. What positive thing can you create for someone today with your words?

1

FRUSTRATION IS MY MOTIVATION

Someone came into my office last week and said, "Ben, I can tell you are frustrated."

Most of the time, we use the word *frustrated* in a negative sense. Certainly the frustration I was feeling was negative at that moment. You might be frustrated with your business, your organization, your marriage, or your children. Frustration can dominate your thinking. Everything is aggravating when seen through the lens of frustration.

Nobody really wants a frustrating life. We all naturally want to have easy relationships. We all want to have ease in our businesses, homes, and careers.

But I want to introduce you to a new perspective on frustration because I believe it is one of the greatest gifts in your life.

Frustration is the precursor to innovation. Frustration can birth vision. Sometimes it is frustration—not necessity—that is the mother of invention. Frustration is a gift.

Here's a word from entrepreneur Jordan Schrandt about the frustration that led to what became a hugely successful business: "When I started realizing the truth about natural living, most of which is covered up or marginalized in American culture, I was blown away by the lack of truth that existed. I was tired of the lack of a prevailing voice in our culture that proclaimed truth about health … and I decided to show up and be a part of that voice. Educating, inspiring, and empowering our generation with how to care for their bodies and their families is my passion."

Frustration is the precursor to innovation.

But frustration needs to be asked certain questions. The people who learn the ability to linger when frustrations arise—to pause, to look frustration in the face and ask these questions—those people start something that matters.

Think about it. There are frustrations littered throughout humanity. Some are more recent, like the frustration we had that our car phone had a cable connected to the car, which meant you couldn't take the phone with you when you got out. Also, the phone was way too big.

Someone sat with frustration and asked it some questions. Isn't there a way to detach the car phone from the cable? Can't we miniaturize these things so I can slip one into my pocket? What stands in the way of making this situation better, and what can we do about these challenges?

I admire the late Josephine Cochrane. In the late 1800s Josephine was frustrated every night when her servants washed her china dishes. It took such a long time, and inevitably breakages would happen.

She had to cope with the frustration, the irritation, the "pain," of broken dishes. Josephine sat and listened to that frustration, sat opposite it at her well-worn table, and asked questions of her frustration. And thankfully frustration coughed up its secrets, and Josephine Cochrane came up with the concept of the dishwasher.[1]

Many of us never think about how someone had to encounter frustration in order for us to enjoy something we now thank the Lord Jesus for every day: our children loading and emptying the dishwasher for us. (Hey, I do it. I know you do too!) We take for granted the work, the pioneer, and even the frustration behind it all, but that frustration led to something amazing.

Thomas Edison also sat across the table from frustration. He, like everyone else around the world at that time, had to sit in the dark every night, dealing with open flames in his home. It frustrated him, but as he interrogated his frustration, what came back was an incredible idea. One might say he had a "light bulb moment." His illumination came because he deliberately sought a response from frustration.[2]

Frustration is the precursor to innovation. So it was with my friend Erin Rodgers, who is one of the greatest communicators I have ever met. I've known Erin for many years. Her husband serves on the board of Hope for Justice, and Erin is a world-class team builder in a wellness company. Her use of social media in building a team is unprecedented. When I interviewed Erin, she had some wonderful insights into how frustration can lead to innovation. Here's what Erin shared.

The start of my career journey was fairly ordinary. While my husband was in law school, I was working in the pharmaceutical industry. I kind of hated my job, but it allowed us to avoid taking on debt for his education. We determined early on that, except for our house, we would stay out of debt as a family. My job wasn't a great fit for me, but it was a great fit for our lives at that time.

After I turned twenty-eight, I went through a season of intense Bible study. During that time I very clearly heard God call me out of pharmaceutical sales and into an inner-city high school to teach math. Suddenly I had to choose between a job I hated that was fantastic in terms of income and flexibility and a job I thought I would love that offered a fraction of the salary and no flexibility whatsoever.

My heart broke for those inner-city kids. The thought that I might be the only adult who spoke kindly to a child that entire week compelled me to take the plunge. My years in that school were a precious time in my life. It was before we had our own kids, so I had a lot of love to give in the classroom.

I went from visiting physicians' offices to sell them on products to teaching in a classroom to sell students on algebra.

After four years we had our first child, and I began to transition out of teaching full time. Then we had another child. I ended up being able to stay home with our two children.

Now, that would be an ideal situation for some people. But I found out very quickly that I am not wired to be a stay-at-home mom. It was definitely not my sweet spot. I'm way more of an achiever, in that I need other things and other people to encourage me, and babies don't do that at all.

I guess I was unknowingly searching for a new way to achieve while also taking care of our family's needs. There came a time when our kids were not healthy, so I set my mind to solving small problems in my house and dove into the world of essential oils. I first got excited about what they could do for our family—solving "mom problems" for the small people in our home, supporting things like better sleep, stronger immune systems, and happier attitudes.

I quickly created a community around essential oils. It was mostly online, but I was so glad to connect people with common concerns. So many people had the same small problems I'd been able to overcome for my kids with these oils.

I started talking about the solutions and products I'd found, and it snowballed from there. Now it's a huge network where we get to help solve some problems of tens of thousands of people every day.

FRUSTRATION IS MY MOTIVATION

You could say that my entire story involves frustration. Originally I was frustrated that my kids weren't well. Then my frustration grew because of some people wanting answers to come to them instead of looking for solutions themselves.

The crazy thing is that frustration in one area of our lives has caused us to grow in ways that actually helped us get through difficult times in other areas of our lives. Funny how that has worked out.

The chief frustration in my life has been when people want me to solve their problems for them. Hey, I'm happy if something I've said solves someone's health dilemma. But I don't want to be everybody's answer guru. I'd much rather equip people to go find the answers for themselves. I'd prefer to show people that they had the ability to solve their own problems all along.

When I'm talking with people who are considering joining my team, I like to say, "You don't need me. Not really. I'm not going to be your problem solver. That's not my job. But I will give you tools. I will show you how you can do it and point you in some directions. And then you can decide if you really want to solve your own problems or not."

I'm interested in having self-solvers on my team. I get frustrated with people who just want to be handed everything. It turned out, years later, that a decision to look for self-solvers is what led our team to be more successful than I imagined.

I have found that leadership is not what people expect it to be. Some people think a leader is the one who goes around directing the way others do their work. I don't agree with this. I'd much rather equip people to be independent thinkers and come up with their own creative solutions.

When someone asks me a question, I could answer them outright. But that's not truly serving the other person. I prefer to say, "You have a question about this? Awesome. Let me talk that out with you. Let's unpack it so you can see that you didn't need me to give you the answer. You had the answer already."

I think really good leaders equip other people to realize that they have it within themselves to figure it out. Practically speaking, it's a whole lot easier and safer to say "I don't know, but let's see if we can find the answer" than it is to try to know all the answers. There's a huge freedom in saying "I don't know." I don't want to feel as if I have to be everything for everybody all the time. That's just being bossy. And I don't want to be bossy.

I want people to be frustrated that they don't know the answer, and I want that frustration to be their motivation to go find out.

One question that has guided my leadership style is this: "Do you want to be an employee or an entrepreneur?" Whether I ask them outright or I observe the way they're behaving, the contrast between these two dispositions will help me understand people's true ability to reach their goals. What I've found is that a lot of people really do want to be an employee. They want the boss to say, "Go do this. Sign up for this. Take these notes. This is how you write this. This is what you say." Employees are great, and the world needs lots of them.

But that's not me, and that's not whom I find achieving the most success on my team. The people I want to work with are those who will watch me do something and then say, "OK, I got it. I'm good. Let me run with it and do it my way."

My strategy is to be like the Wizard of Oz. I like to peel back the curtain a little and show people what's happening. Sometimes they run off and do something totally differently than how I would do it. That used to bother me a lot. But then I realized it was what I'd been wanting the whole time. I had to say, "Oh, wait. That's actually good. No, you're fine. Go do your thing."

It's possible that their own way will fail—but that's fine too. They'll learn from that failure if they're really going to succeed. And maybe they'll invent a new way that's even better than how I'm doing it, and I'll start doing it their way!

Let Leaders Arise on Their Own

No matter how many people you have on your team, only a fraction of them will ever rise up as leaders who really succeed. And you don't know who it will be.

I am hopeful for everyone who joins our organization, and I desire success for each person—both in their health choices and in the industry. I firmly believe everyone can be successful. Over the years I've had many friends link arms with us. Some have caught the vision and run with it. Others didn't have the same goals for themselves that I saw for them, and that is hard.

I concentrate now on loving my people well and keeping an eye out for those on my team who love the product. Those are the ones who will become leaders. I have learned to quit pushing people into a role of leadership or into business. I had to quit dreaming for them. If they're not yet willing to dream and they're not yet able to see an opportunity, I cannot open their eyes for them. There is far more success when I let leaders emerge on their own.

When Things Get Difficult

I talked earlier about how my frustration led to a practice of look-ing for team builders who didn't sit around waiting on me to give them the answers and how that led to them increasing our team's success. Here's what I meant.

I'd have to say that 2018 was the hardest year for me. I was dealing with a number of personal issues that had me feeling up and down already, but then in July my husband and I found out I was pregnant. This was a shock, as we already had two active children, ages five and seven, and we had considered ourselves done having kids. However, the surprise finally wore off, and right as I was starting to feel like myself again, I miscarried.

It was a really hard time for our family. And while that year strengthened us in a lot of ways, I'm thrilled it is behind us.

During that time I was overwhelmed. I was neck deep in run-ning a successful business with tens of thousands of people on my team. You should've seen my inbox, and don't get me started about the social marketing work I was doing. I was loving life, being that busy and involved. But when all this fell down on us, I couldn't keep up with it all. I had to step back.

I was concerned that if I did pull away, the whole thing would come to a screeching halt. That was kind of unrealistic, now that I think about it, but I had the fear that any drop in my own involvement would mean a catastrophic collapse of my whole organization. I had to find out whether I had done a good job as leader and had put systems and people in place that would keep us successful if I was not 100 percent on my game.

I found that I had already entrusted people on my team with leadership. I hadn't intentionally done this as a way of taking care of the organization in case I wasn't present—though I probably should have! But through my style of leading, I had cared for my team well, so in a moment when I had to step back, I was able to say, "Hey, guys, I gotta deal with some stuff. I'm going to go quiet for a while. Can you guys step in and do what needs to be done?" And they did. Beautifully.

Sometimes I didn't even have the energy to tell my team I was having to duck away. I was just suddenly gone, and they knew what was going on and were able to step in.

If you empower the people around you and gather to yourself people who don't need you sitting over them telling them what to do, you will build a robust leadership structure that can carry on quite nicely without you.

Now, if people want to have everything fall apart if they're not there holding the reins, they should definitely not empower their people. But strong organizations that can endure the hard times are those that can function well if the primary leadership is not there—even for an extended time, as in my case.

I also realized that my absence was good on so many levels. For one thing, it showed my team leaders that they were every bit as good at doing these things as I was, which encouraged them even more.

It was also good for me to start modeling more of what I had been teaching others. I came to see that if I'm teaching how to thrive with family, then sometimes I needed to step away from the business to go thrive with my family. If I was teaching them to find a passion outside their business, then at times I really needed to be off pursuing other passions besides growing the business. It wasn't my intention to start modeling that in 2018, but events forced me to do so, and it was a powerful message to my team.

My original motivation years ago was a frustration with my kids' health. That led to me creating a business selling essential oils, and my frustration with the "employee" attitude led me to gather a team of people who were, basically, already leaders. That intentional direction had a quite unlooked-for outcome for me: those people stepped even further into their leadership roles just when I needed them to have my back. If I had surrounded myself with people who needed to be told what to do, they never could've taken up the slack for me when I had to be away. Frustration was my motivation, but it also became my salvation in that season.

To Those Tempted to Quit

If you're thinking of quitting and you confess this to a business leader, the most likely response will be something along the lines of finding endurance or pressing through to the other side. Perhaps even something like "You should never quit."

But I'm not sure that's the right answer. It's definitely not the answer I would give. I mean, I've quit several things in my life. I quit my job as a pharmaceutical sales rep, after all. A few years later, I quit my job teaching math in an inner-city school. I quit being a full-time stay-at-home mom. I never really thought of those as quitting, though, at least not in the sense of running away from something when it got difficult.

There are seasons when we have to *readjust*, and I think that's really healthy. Some things I've done were a good fit for a time but then were not. Why keep doing something that isn't working if there's no compelling reason to keep doing it? If there is a compelling reason, then maybe you need to sit down and evaluate what is making you want to quit. Maybe you need to adjust to your situation and pursue the same goal in a different way. Maybe it's time to shift to a new goal.

I once read a book about the walls we run into in our lives. Some walls are made of things we need to keep pounding against until we find a way to break through them. Other walls are going to break our bones, so we ought to change our paths. No one can tell you which kind of wall you're up against. You have to determine that for yourself.

Many times the thing you want to quit doing is actually a very good and noble thing, but it's simply not the right time for you to be doing it. That can make the decision tough. Yes, this is a good thing, but is it going to get us to our dreams?

If you're facing a wall right now, ask yourself how badly you want what's on the other side of it. That answer may be different at different times in your life, even for the same goal. Something you wanted badly ten years ago may not matter as much now. Your priorities may have shifted, and that's OK. It's good to let go of goals that don't need to be at the top of your list any longer. You don't have infinite energy or time, so make sure you're spending what you do have on the goals you most treasure.

If that means quitting on one or more goals to pursue your highest one, give yourself permission to do that.

But if you find that the goal on the other side of the wall is in fact what you most want to reach, then keep working to get there. Bring in new people; get new ideas; surrender all your old approaches; be willing to change tactics entirely. The goal, after all, is the goal. If you have to change strategies or paths in order to get there, that's OK.

You may decide that the thing on the other side of this wall is what you want, but your heart is tired, your head is weary, and you just need a nap. But after that nap you're going to power through that wall.

Reevaluating is important, though. Some paths are just not right for you. Not for now or not forever. I was not meant to be a pharmaceutical rep for twenty years. That was not my calling. But we needed the money at that time in our lives, and I could have stuck with it if I'd had to. I'm so glad I didn't. I'm so glad I listened to the voices that were saying, *Hey, you'd be a great teacher. You'd be really great at helping people understand things, and you also have a gift for mathematics.*

Where are your dreams? Where are you trying to go? Don't quit just because it's hard or because you've hit a wall or you need a nap. But definitely take the time to stop and reevaluate the direction you're headed. It's never a bad time to ask yourself whether you're still pointed in the right direction. If you determine that you are going the right way but there is a wall in the way, focus on how you're going to get through (or around or under or over) that wall.

When you reevaluate, you may find that your life is coming together like a puzzle. I mean, I can look at the medical science I learned from the pharmaceutical job and see how that enabled me to perceive how essential oils were working inside the body. That made me a great proponent of the product and a great teacher and educator. The science also told me what I never wanted to put in my body or in my children.

The science and math helped me as a teacher, and the teaching in turn gave me the confidence to stand in front of a group and present something. Now I regularly stand before thousands of people and talk to them about health and wellness.

Every step in my life got me to where I am today—even the things I "quit" and the hard times I had to walk through. Every one of those played a role in where I am.

Look at your own life. Can you see how the major events and experiences—even the hardships—have sculpted you into the person you are now? Can you see how they have given you certain passions and made you rise up to defend certain causes? The good you're doing in the world now is a result of what you've been through, good and bad, and even the things you've stopped doing.

Friends in Other Places

I have learned that you have to have some really close friends you don't work with.

For one thing, if you're really successful in your business, it's great to have people in your life who don't know you that way. They just know you as Erin who drives the car pool and is sometimes late. It really keeps you grounded, especially if you spend a lot of your time in circles where you're seen as the boss.

For another, having friends you don't work with can really help when you're not being terribly successful in business. They don't know you as that person who is crashing emotionally because she didn't hit her goal this month. They just know you as their favorite movie-loving friend.

If all your friends are your employees or your bosses or they are your trainers or team members, you may find yourself very lonely.

That was my experience a few years ago. I intentionally found friends who weren't in the business with me. I needed people I could be raw and real and silly with. Creating some space for that sort of friendship really helped me. It's with those people that I can go so much deeper.

As I look back over my career—my many careers—I see that frustration really has been my motivation. I still get frustrated, but in good ways. If I don't know how to do something, I love learning how to do it. I think adjusting to new technology has been one of my secrets not only of success but also of staying fresh and growing.

What are you frustrated about? Can it become something that motivates you to get up and do something about it? If you're an entrepreneur, your frustration probably has already spurred you upward and outward. Necessity is the mother of invention, but frustration is the mother of change.

May frustration always propel you to create good in the world, and may you find peace in whom you have been made to be.

Frustration is not a quick fix. As we saw in Erin's story, it takes time. It takes energy. But instead of ignoring the problem or passing the buck, Erin and the others featured in this book considered their frustration a precursor to innovation. They lingered in the conversation. They committed. And many are the beneficiaries of their choices.

Frustration is a constant in your world. Accept it. You will encounter frustration at every stage of the journey. Consider it a gift that is trying to tell you exactly what innovation it has for you.

Momentum is fueled by both an acceptance of and an engagement with frustration. Don't get frustrated with frustration. Let the frustration be a helpful bit of coaching, letting you know to keep looking for the best way to do what you are trying to do. Sit down with frustration. Write the questions you want frustration to answer.

As I've said, the best leaders ask the best questions. But here's the corollary: the best entrepreneurs—the world changers—ask questions of *frustration*. They sit at that well-worn table until the job is done.

Kevin Kim understands the connection between pain and triumph. Kevin is an embodiment of a line in a poem: "The [lesson] you deliver may be very wise and true, / But I'd rather get my lessons by observing what you do."[3] I'm so grateful he's spoken into this book:

Think about the lives of some of the most beautiful and inspirational people you know and ask yourself whether a tree of that height and magnificence can dispense with seasons of harsh winters and storms. They didn't achieve their greatness by avoiding pain and suffering or even despite it—they achieved because of it.

Dr. Martin Luther King Jr., in his book *Strength to Love*, quoted a biographer of George Frideric Handel: "His health and his fortunes had reached the lowest ebb. His right side had become paralyzed, and his money was all gone. His creditors seized him and threatened him with imprisonment. For a brief time he was tempted to give up the fight—but then he rebounded again to compose the greatest of his inspirations, the epic *Messiah*." Then Dr. King wrote, "The 'Hallelujah Chorus' was born, not in a sequestered villa in Spain, but in a narrow, undesirable cell."[4]

King reminded us that our greatest achievements are inextricably linked to our greatest pains. Put another way, the cliché that nothing great is easy and nothing easy becomes great is actually true. Ask any leader, any artist, any person who has achieved, and that person will tell you that in the interval between initial failure and subsequent success, in the gap between who someone is and who he or she could be, is pain and suffering.

As you read this, you may be staring frustration in the eyes. Like many others, you may be tackling the biggest frustrations and asking the really big questions: Why are children being exploited? What can we do to end poverty? How do we solve world hunger? How do we eradicate corruption? How do we mend a broken economy? How do we bring compassion back into capitalism? How do we address immorality in complex supply chains? How do we make financial markets fair? How do we solve the world's environmental crisis?

Maybe your biggest frustration is closer to home. Maybe it's something to do with your primary relationships or your living situation or your health.

What are you sitting around that table asking? What is your frustration?

All those years ago, when I walked out of that building in Manchester, something was different inside me. Oh, I'd heard many other people talking about legitimate and important causes around the world, but I'd never been moved to do something personally. That night I dared to ask, *What can I do about modern slavery?*

As I asked that question, I found answers beginning to come. Because I lingered.

The answers will come for you as well. I have learned to see frustration not only as a motivation to find solutions, not only as a precursor to innovation, but also as my friend.

I still have frustrations. I'm frustrated that there are still people trapped in slavery. I'm frustrated that our team is not yet large enough. I'm frustrated that we're not operating in as many countries as I would like. I'm frustrated that our income is not at the levels I want it to be.

See how many "friends" are helping us to our goal?

The moment I lose my frustration is the moment I do the thing I should never do: settle. Settle for what I have. Settle for the impact we have made in the past. Settle for the status quo. Settle for the fact that some people remain enslaved.

Innovation cannot arise from settling. Nothing is created by just setting up camp where you are. You need momentum.

Start thinking about how your frustration can start bringing solutions.

Frustration is your greatest gift. It can be the precursor to innovation and the genesis of your life's vision.

DISCUSSION QUESTIONS

1. What frustration are you currently facing? What have you not fixed yet? Write down those frustrations.
2. What are you going to do about those frustrations?
3. Who in your world can help?

INNOVATION IS AN INVITATION

If you want to be successful, you have to innovate constantly.

Frustration, as we've seen, is often the precursor to change. But frustration is just the beginning. One of the reasons frustration persists in the world is that no good *solution* has yet been devised for the thing that is causing it. Frustration alone, if the problem is approached in the same ways it has been approached over the years, won't result in change.

Arthur Schopenhauer, a German philosopher in the 1800s, once said that to make a great discovery or innovation, "the problem is not so much to see what nobody has yet seen, as to think what nobody has yet thought."[1]

I used to think if I could just come up with one amazing idea, it would change the world. It's absolutely true. One idea can change the world. But one of the greatest lessons I've learned is that innovation is required too. The need for innovation is a constant.

We live in a day and age when innovation is happening at an unprecedented rate. Think about how technology has evolved over the last forty years. I grew up when mobile phones were just being invented. My father's friend had a mobile phone in his car. It was huge, and it was attached to a wire, but I thought, *Wow, what will they do next?*

My first mobile phone was a Nokia 3210, and I was thrilled. If you are under the age of thirty, you probably won't know what I'm talking about, but the screen of this phone was green. This phone was so innovative that it actually had a color screen. I didn't know how they made it green, but I was amazed. What's more, the phone actually vibrated when it rang. I mean, you could feel someone calling even when the phone was in your pocket. That phone was a modern-day miracle.

Fast-forward twenty years, and mobile phones have developed tremendously. We play games on them as if they're gaming consoles. We take high-resolution photos with them better than many cameras. We use our phones to connect with the world through social media and email. We use them as boarding passes for flights.

When it comes to mobile phone technology, innovation has been happening nonstop. In technology of all kinds, if you're not innovating, if you're just standing still, you're going backward.

The same is true in all areas of your life. It's not just in the realm of technology or business or medicine. Innovation keeps an organization alive.

Jen Jordan is another very successful entrepreneurial friend. She says that constantly innovating, growing, and learning new things is part of what keeps her alive: "It's crazy that the techniques I used to grow my business, even six years ago, are largely irrelevant today. When it comes to technology and social media, if you don't learn the new thing, you're going to get left behind. This younger generation is always wanting to do new things, so if you want to reach them, you'd better take the jump with them. But learning these new things has brought me life. It's great to be learning something new and be challenged to figure it out."

When I started Hope for Justice, I did so because there was a great need. But I also found a unique selling point. We were in the glorious position of being first to market, and we were going to provide a service that no one else had provided. The services we brought were fresh and unique then.

But if I were starting out today, in the current social justice landscape, the things we did then wouldn't work now. We would be irrelevant. We would not be needed. Since those early days when we were first into the modern slavery space, the landscape has changed. We have had to evaluate and innovate constantly.

Both frustration and innovation will always be in your life—and they need to be. When you harness the two, you will do well.

I often quote this to our team: "The pessimist complains about the wind. The optimist expects it to change. The leader adjusts the sails."[2]

What things do you need to adjust the sails on? Where do you need to go? What needs to change about your product or your organization?

Some of us are using outdated concepts in a world that has changed on us. What's your idea that's beyond current ideas? What questions are you asking about what you are doing, how you are handling things, and what needs to be updated and improved?

Sir Brian Souter is one of the most gifted leaders I've ever met. And he's a big, longtime supporter of Hope for Justice. He has developed businesses and sat at tables of influencers across the world. He has shaped how business looks in the UK and around the world. Not only is he one of the most successful businessmen I have ever met, but he is also fundamentally one of the humblest men I've ever met.

My father was a bus driver, and I worked as a student bus conductor. Since I was young, I have been quite passionate about public transport. But even then, when I was young and working in a state-owned company, I would see things that I thought could be done differently or better. When the government deregulated the long-distance bus industry and privatized all such companies, I saw it as an opportunity to have a go at doing it myself.

What I identified was a niche in the market for intercity travel in Scotland. Before, such a thing wasn't really available. When the oil boom was in its heyday, I had worked for an accountant in Aberdeen, and I had seen how difficult it was to get to Aberdeen from the major Scottish cities if you didn't have your own car. I had the idea that this was actually an opportunity to provide a bus service to there. Since it was a long distance, I had the further idea to provide food on the buses, which had never been done before. That proved to be very successful, and it led to everything that came after.

I think I got the entrepreneurial gene from my father. He'd always be doing different things when I was young: buying and selling cars, renting properties, and pursuing all sorts of other business interests. I think he gave us that crazy streak to see an opportunity, have an idea, and have a go at things. I always seemed to be able to see a challenge and have an idea ... though some of my ideas were terrible.

I think what makes an entrepreneur is not only having an idea but also having the courage to implement it. So many people have great ideas, but they can't or won't get off their backsides and do them. You have to have both.

I had the idea of providing intercity and long-distance busing in Scotland back in 1980. I had saved £12,000 ($15,500), which was not an insignificant amount at that time. My father put £25,000 ($32,300) into the business, which was a very big amount. And my sister went to the bank and increased the borrowing against her house, which was a pretty gutsy thing to do. That gave us another £12,000 or so, and we pooled all that capital to grow the business.

One might think that having us all extending ourselves like this would cause awkward conversations around the dinner table. But we had very good relationships with one another and recognized the risks. My father was a silent investor, but what he was really doing was backing his kids. The old family business philosophy.

INNOVATION IS AN INVITATION

Ben says, "Innovation is an invitation," and that's certainly true. I conflate that with the idea of an opportunity you see. I might say that the opportunity, or the niche, you see is the invitation. Then your idea of how to innovate is part of what you bring to the opportunity.

When we started our bus service, we saw a need (to get to Aberdeen on public transport) and an opportunity (to do what no one else was doing and what people needed). The other part of the opportunity was that the government changed the legislation, allowing for the rise of private transport companies. A couple of opportunities presented themselves, and that was an invitation for us to bring our innovative solution.

There are other times when you realize that the market itself is changing, and that brings opportunity. The introduction of Megabus, our internet-based bus company, is a good example of this.

When the internet boom happened twenty-plus years ago, everyone was asking, "How do you monetize this web thing? How do you turn this into a business?" The market had invented a new way of doing business, which meant there was vast opportunity to anyone who could see how to use it. We managed to reinvent a long-distance bus service and turn it into one that did business over the internet. Entrepreneurs are constantly looking at where they can innovate and keep ahead of the changes.

Entrepreneurs see a challenge or a setback as an opportunity too. More recently the government has implemented emissions regulations that have had a tremendous impact on buses, lorries, trains, and more. Some businessmen I know have been rather put back because of these changes, but we saw them as an opportunity.

We decided that if we could quickly invest in updating our fleet, we could be approved—and perhaps be the first or only one approved—to operate in heritage sectors like Cambridge and Edinburgh. The new emissions laws showed us exactly how to innovate to gain a competitive advantage.

We have found in our own market research that people don't want to use a dirty product. More and more, people in the UK are moving away from using individual cars and moving toward public transport—and those who have shifted to public transport have a strong sensitivity about the environment. If we are out there not only with one bus replacing twenty private vehicles but with clean buses, we clearly stand out and appeal to the mood of the times.

One innovation we're quite proud of has to do with our workforce. I've noticed that there is a divide between employees of one generation and the next. Those interacting across the parent-child age range often have difficulty working together. Sometimes it seems as if the parent-aged group sees young people as a threat, and this suppresses innovation.

So we try to hire according to a grandparent-grandchild type of arrangement. I've always felt that having a mixture of young people who have the skills, particularly related to the revolution in technology, and older people who have experience is a good combination for us. I think that intergenerational mix, when it works well, can be really good because the older people are seasoned and the younger people have the skills. Older people don't usually see younger workers as a threat—they just see them as interesting and enjoy working with them. That's proved really successful for us.

The innovation that I'm proudest of or that would be considered the biggest achievement would be consolidating the UK bus companies. Years ago, we took in some new investors and hoovered up some sixty transport companies and consolidated them all into what is now Stagecoach. That was a massive undertaking and landscape change.

But I get ideas for innovation all the time. And I quite like investing in new start-ups all around the world. I just recently sold businesses in Poland and Finland that we had developed. I enjoy introducing some of those new products and working in countries overseas.

When Things Get Difficult

I find it most challenging when my normal ability to work well with almost everyone is overcome and I realize I'm at an impasse.

As a rule, I try my best to salvage even the most difficult business relationships. If someone who works for you has skill sets you want or brings something you can work with, you do your best to work it out with that person.

Unfortunately some people are simply impossible to work with. It doesn't matter what you do; they will always end up with enormous chips on their shoulders because of the nature of their personalities. In those rare times, if in my conscience I know I have given them a fair chance, a couple of opportunities, some good advice, and it still doesn't work, I just have to get on with it and move on. It is never easy, but it has to be done.

And sometimes, especially in an investment, you come across some people who are just not fit to run the business. It's hard, but you have to move them out and make changes. In that case, I try to make it clear that it's not personal, I explain what the issues are, and I do it as humanely as possible.

To Those Tempted to Quit

It depends on the situation. I have spoken with people whose businesses are simply not going to make it. Maybe it's endemic or structural or something else, but it won't matter how hard they try; they're not going to make it. To be honest, in that circumstance they are smart to cut and run.

However, if you have a great idea and there are signs it is going to be successful, then persevere, by all means!

But deciding which situation applies to you is a judgment only you can make.

The Lowest Point

When you've been in business as long as I have, you've been through many low points. Financial, emotional, and fear-filled low points can challenge you from all sides.

We went through a phase years ago when we made a big error with an acquisition in North America. It really imploded on us. I think the share price fell to nine pence (twelve cents) at one point. Now, even in the middle of that, I had a firm conviction—or what you might call peace—that it was going to come through and everything would be OK in the end. And it was. But that was probably the most difficult point.

And then, in the early days of the company, we found that we were overtrading and really short of capital. At one point I thought we were going to go bust. That was the scariest time.

That was one of those occasions when having a strong faith proved an advantage. First I was worried almost beyond my ability to function, and then I surrendered it. I realized that if we came through it, it would be God's will. And if we didn't come through it, that would be God's will as well, and at least it would be a good learning experience. When I finally got to that point of surrender, I experienced a real peace about the situation.

Help came from an unlooked-for source, actually. Back then the railway industry in the UK had a very strong trade union. In the middle of our crisis, they went on strike for two months. During that time, if you were going to travel around Scotland at all, you had to get on a Stagecoach bus. That really helped.

Some Innovations for Challenging Times

Innovation is an invitation. Opportunity is an invitation. Challenges and setbacks are invitations. And even failure and great opposition can be invitations.

Here are some more practices I have found useful in my businesses. Perhaps a moment when you're facing challenges is your invitation to try some new things—to innovate. And these might be some you try on for size.

First, I think it's quite important that you build a philosophy, not an empire of directives. Other people call this creating the culture you wish to have in your organization or celebrating what you want to replicate. Once you have built a philosophy you share with other people in the business, you don't have to stand over people or micromanage, because you know they are going to do the right things. You know they are going to understand what the objectives are and what the principles are in the business. I think that is very important in leadership, because your people all take their cues from you.

Second, it's essential to be committed to a very open and honest way of doing business. We did this long before it was fashionable. We never participated in bribery overseas, despite the fact that our competitors did this and despite the fact that opting out of bribery caused us to lose at least one major contract. The UK has enacted new anticorruption legislation over the past ten years, but it didn't make any difference to us, because we were already operating that way.

Third, we have always kept a short chain of command. That has been one of my strategic principles from the beginning. If you run the company so everybody understands where they stand within the chain of command and what their responsibilities are, the right decisions can be made all up and down the chain of command. And the shorter that chain of command, the more efficient the business. Even with the size of Stagecoach, we never allowed more than four links in the chain of command between the individual bus driver and the chief executive.

Fourth, and this won't be appropriate for everyone, but I do think there is an advantage when the leader has faith. Your faith brings you a consistency, and when things are as they should be, it means that you are not building everything to prove your worth. It's so difficult to work with people who feel they have to prove their importance, their superiority, or their value. They're trying to force this sense of confidence all the time, because it is all about them. Leaders who have found their worth in Christ have different dimensions. They are not worried about getting ahead or sabotaging others or being impressive. When they understand that their personal lives are in God's hands and they don't have to prove anything to anyone, they can concentrate on being faithful and doing what's right.

Faith is a big help in terms of how you cope with things. The stress levels in your life are greatly reduced when you don't have to worry about the self-image that drives and motivates so many people.

John Burroughs is credited with saying, "The smallest deed is better than the greatest intention."[3] Many people get frustrated by something in the world and realize they need to innovate, so they have every intention of doing so. But that's where they stop. Many people walk out of conference centers or churches or motivational speeches with the greatest of intentions about what they're going to do next.

Great. Intention is good. But it's not enough. At some point you have to start acting so innovation can happen. Don't stay stuck in your intention of *I'm going to change something.*

Intention, if it never proceeds to action, is a campsite.

How many world-changing ideas haven't come to fruition because the people who had them didn't move to the next stage? Rather than a campsite, intention should become an active state of strategic progression. Innovation is the engine that moves you from frustration and intention to the work of turning your goal into reality.

I want to challenge you to memorize this formula:

frustration + innovation = changing the world

Kevin Kim recalls how desperation led to innovation for the founders of Airbnb:

> When Airbnb started, Joe Gebbia and Brian Chesky were struggling just to make rent. They had an idea to come up with a solution for people who couldn't stay in hotels because they were fully booked or too expensive. The idea was to rent air beds on their living room floor to guests for eighty dollars and cook them breakfast in the morning. They created the website airbedandbreakfast.com, and they were off and running.
>
> In the summer of 2008, they had the perfect kick start for their fledgling business. Barack

Obama was going to speak in Denver at the Democratic National Convention, and many people were going to need places to stay. Gebbia and Chesky relaunched their website two weeks before the conference. But the website wasn't making any money. In order to keep the company going, they sold cereal. That's right—they sold cereal to survive. They purchased huge quantities of cereal, designed cardboard boxes, and branded them as limited-edition, politically themed cereal like Obama's O's and Cap'n McCain's in order to raise money. This netted them a little over thirty thousand dollars to put into their business.[4]

Innovation is an invitation. A closed door is a challenge to find a new one to walk through.

DISCUSSION QUESTIONS

1. In what areas do you need to think differently, to innovate, to shift?
2. What innovations have inspired you? Why?
3. What environment do you need to create to regain innovation or sustain the innovation process?

RESPONSIBILITY IS AN OPPORTUNITY

Former British prime minister Winston Churchill once said, "The price of greatness is responsibility."[1] I quite like that, and I've found it to be true. If you want to do great things in the world, you have to be willing to take on responsibility. The responsibility and the opportunity to achieve greatness are linked.

Through leading Hope for Justice, I have come to realize that the people I can most depend on, the ones I can trust most, are those who understand the opportunity of responsibility. They are the people who "own their zone," as my friend Charlotte Gambill would say.

There is something incredibly attractive about a team member, a family member, a friend, or anyone else who owns his or her actions and understands the opportunity inherent in responsibility.

I was recently in Poipet, visiting some of our team in Cambodia. I have seen poverty all around the world. But around our office in Poipet, I saw poverty at another level. The smells, the sights, and the sheer lack were overwhelming.

Our office is situated right in the middle of what is basically a wasteland. We are there to help potential victims of modern slavery who are escaping to Cambodia across the Thai border. As I walked toward our office, I was literally stepping through human feces, broken glass, animal excrement, and I shudder to think what else. But this was our outpost here, and in the few weeks before my visit, they had rescued twenty-two individuals from slavery. So I slogged on.

I got to the front door and met the staff. They urged me to come inside, and because of what I'd seen so far, I expected the office to be as derelict and dirty as everything around it.

But when I stepped inside, I found the office absolutely spotless.

In that moment I realized that the leader and team at this office were people who understood the opportunity of responsibility. These staff members owned their zone. They had said to themselves, *Yes, the surrounding environment may be challenging. But if we are going to be a place where we welcome those just rescued from modern slavery, we want them to find order, peace, comfort, and cleanliness.*

How many of us look at the external circumstances in our lives and blame them for who we are? *I am like this because of that person. I am like this because of this bank account. I am like this because of my education. I am like this because of my upbringing.*

I don't mean to sound insensitive, and I don't want to minimize your experiences, but let me say this: your "because of" could be the biggest barrier to your greatness.

If you want to be great, you have to own everything in your life. Take responsibility for yourself. There is great opportunity in responsibility.

Your thinking is up to you. Stop blaming people and experiences. Your attitude is up to you. Your behavior is up to you. Your life is up to you. Yes, bad things may have happened, but it's up to you whether you let them be an excuse for not living the life you want.

Your opportunity in life is up to you, and it all hinges on whether you're willing to take responsibility. If you want to pursue your impossible, if you want to have momentum, you need to create movement through responsibility.

Dr. Robi Sonderegger is, without doubt, one of the premier psychologists in the world. He's a personal friend, and I've looked up to him for many years. We once accidentally climbed a mountain together in Switzerland. He told me we were going for a short walk, and five hours later, I was on top of the mountain, still wearing a sports jacket.

He is also incredibly humble, a gifted communicator, and one of the most thoughtful and helpful psychologists in terms of dealing with trauma and victims of trauma.

He definitely understands that responsibility is an opportunity, but if you ever get to meet Dr. Robi, do not go on a walk with him.

My team of clinical psychologists and I work around the world on the front lines of natural disasters and in areas of civil conflict and war. Increasingly we've been working with people who have been rescued out of human trafficking or sexual exploitation. Trauma is the umbrella category. Since high-impact life events can leave a person traumatized, we've been helping rehabilitate people in this domain for the last fifteen years.

More recently we've noticed that some people do more than just make a recovery. Some go from strength to strength and end up better off than how they were before the tragedy. This has interested us.

In their cases the old adage is true that what doesn't kill you makes you stronger. But we've found through our research that this applies to only a small group of people. For most people, that which doesn't kill you *almost* killed you, and you walk around with a limp for the rest of your life because you've been so affected by your past. The vast majority of people, perhaps especially in Western cultures, are not made stronger by tragedy or hardship.

But some are.

We have come to recognize that our past can either *define* us or *refine* us. Those who are refined by their trauma, who truly end up being better off, are experiencing what scientific literature calls posttraumatic *growth*.[2] Everyone's heard of posttraumatic stress disorder, but posttraumatic growth is when people actually use their hardship as a springboard and a catalyst to improve their lives.

RESPONSIBILITY IS AN OPPORTUNITY

If it's true that your past can either define you or refine you, what determines which way it goes? We have found that it depends on the person's choice. It's been said that no one can offend you without your permission, and I believe that's true. No one can destroy your life and leave you emotionally paralyzed without your participation. The one who decides whether a tragedy gets the better of you or becomes a stepping-stone to your growth is ... you.

Those who see setbacks as springboards end up going places they would previously never have dreamed of going, all because of great tragedy. For us it is incredibly exciting to see traumatized people realizing this on the different front lines around the world. People harmed by war, conflict, abuse, rape, torture, injustice, and trafficking are grasping that they don't have to let what has been done to them define the rest of their lives.

We are equally passionate about taking this sort of front-lines psychology back to the home front. Uganda and Iraq are not the only places where people are traumatized. Sometimes we can look over our neighbor's fence or listen through the wall to the apartment next door, and it sounds like a war zone there too. No matter where the abuse or disaster takes place, we all need to learn these life lessons.

When something terrible is done to us, of course healing must happen. And though we don't understand it in these terms at the time, being the receiver of trauma gives us both a responsibility and an opportunity. We have the responsibility of choosing whether we are going to turn inward and become stuck and bitter and see our entire identity as a victim or we're going to let the trauma teach us and cause us to grow.

When we take responsibility and refuse to succumb to self-pity, a great, yawning opportunity opens before us like the mouth of an enormous natural cavern. The person whose identity becomes that of a victim will never find that cavern. Responsibility brings remarkable opportunity.

The only qualification you need to have in order to be marginalized, betrayed, hard done by (or treated badly), offended, or victimized is simply to be born. Everyone goes through hardships. It's not *if* but **when**. It's not **Why me?** but **What took it so long?** But we don't have to stay in the posture of a victim.

Case in point is Joseph from the Old Testament. Joseph was betrayed and sold into slavery by his own brothers. He was purchased by an Egyptian and worked faithfully but then was betrayed by his boss's wife—for the "crime" of *not* being immoral. He was sent to prison unjustly. While in prison, he interpreted dreams for prisoners and asked that one remember him when he was released. But that man completely forgot about Joseph (see Gen. 37, 39-40).

Joseph's betrayals and hardships came one after the other. But you never get the sense that he was sitting back in his cell feeling sorry for himself. He used each setback as a learning opportunity to forge his leadership. If it hadn't been for those hardships, he never would have been able to oversee and lead the nation when he finally did get out of prison.

How do we use the setbacks in our lives? If we can see them more as step-**ups** than setbacks, we will be well served. Each hardship, each tragedy, is an opportunity to choose whether to get smaller or to get larger. To let it kill us or to let it make us stronger.

The Responsibility and Opportunity for Healthy Thinking

I believe healthy thinking looks very different from how people think it looks. My observation is that people see healthy thinking as *positive* thinking. We're living in the age of self-affirmation and your best life now. But some of that can be quite unhealthy thinking, in my view. True healthy thinking goes so much deeper than just positive thinking.

In my opinion, healthy thinking is *intentional* thinking. I love this Bible passage: "Do not be anxious about anything, but in every situation, by prayer and petition, with thanksgiving, present your requests to God. And the peace of God, which transcends all understanding, will guard your hearts and your minds in Christ Jesus. Finally, brothers and sisters, whatever is true, whatever is noble, whatever is right, whatever is pure, whatever is lovely, whatever is admirable—if anything is excellent or praiseworthy—think about such things" (Phil. 4:6-8).

The writer, Paul, laid out this pathway for us. It starts with not being anxious, and it ends with meditating on what is right, pure, and good. That's not just positive thinking—it's intentional, disciplined thinking. Healthy thinking is less about being positive and more about being intentional. And that requires *autonomy*.

Autonomy, in my mind, is basically taking responsibility. It's the opposite of blaming. It's the opposite of a victim mind-set. Autonomy sees the opportunity within responsibility and says, "I'm not only grateful for the opportunities I have; I'm also going to seize my power and go make the life I wish to have."

Some people say that social media is unhealthy from a psychological or emotional perspective, but I disagree. It can be unhealthy, but it's not necessarily so. Just because someone posts something good doesn't mean you have to go into depression about it. It's not about what someone posts but about how secure we are on the inside.

We could look at a post and think, *Well, praise the Lord! How wonderful that this person is sharing their highlights. Each one is a testimony to God's goodness in their life!* Someone else could look at the same post and think, *I'm jealous about that. They don't deserve that. How dare they? It's just a reminder that I'm not good enough. I wish I had that wife or that car or that job.* Social media isn't healthy or unhealthy. What's healthy or unhealthy is your thinking and your feelings about yourself.

The person with healthy thinking thinks, *Wow, I do want a car and a job and a wife like that. And I know I can have the things I want. I have the opportunity to take responsibility for what I want and start working toward it.*

People with autonomy realize that the gray matter between their ears is the most valuable asset they have and improving it is the best investment they could possibly make. Those people think, *If I harness this asset I've been given, I can be hope filled. I can look forward to a great tomorrow.*

But most people in our society today don't have autonomy. They'd rather blame and be victims. They'd rather think, *I am being marginalized. I'm being hard done by.* It doesn't take much to get offended these days. Everybody's a victim.

A sense of entitlement always follows the victim mind-set. "I deserve more!" Which usually leads to self-indulgence, which in turn leads to self-deception and broken relationships—which end up reinforcing the feeling of being a victim. It's just a downward spiral.

It's within your power, you know. You're choosing, one way or the other. Why not choose to take responsibility and stop the blaming?

When Things Get Difficult

In my line of work, I deal with the darkest parts of humanity. I talk with people who have been victimized in the most tragic, brutal ways humankind can devise. Of course, there is deep healing that has to take place, and we have many ways to move in that direction. But for most of us, a surprisingly important part of "keeping on with a hard row to hoe" is maintaining healthy habits.

A simple way to maintain healthy habits is to remember the five *R* words: *renew, rage, relate, revive,* and *restore.*

Renew. I've heard it said that leaders are readers. But I disagree, mainly because I prefer audiobooks over reading! I'd say leaders are *learners*. We must renew our minds on an ongoing basis, like Romans 12:2 says: "Do not conform to the pattern of this world, but be transformed by the renewing of your mind." Often we misinterpret that and think, *OK, I'll just snap out of this and think positively.* No, it's a daily discipline to keep learning and to keep renewing our minds.

Rage. We have to rage for our souls. We have to make sure we're not growing weary in our souls, because that's when people fall morally. So we want to go out and have intentional fun. Good, healthy fun as opposed to the unhealthy variety.

Relate. We must be intentional about relating well. That's why we must prioritize relationships and family over finance.

Revive. It's important that we revive our spirits by spending time with God. Billy Graham, toward the end of his life, was asked whether he would change anything if he could do it all over again. He said, "I would pray more, travel less."[3] That's killing me right now because I'm still traveling way too much. We need to revive our spirits and make sure there's discipline there.

Restore. The final discipline is to restore our bodies. I once heard of a famous Scottish pastor from the 1800s who, on his deathbed and speaking of his failing body, said, "God gave me a message to deliver and a horse to ride. Alas, I have killed the horse and now I cannot deliver the message."[4] We want to make sure we don't do that!

Here are four more *R* words for healthy living: *run, raw, rest,* and *reflect.*

Run. Take care of your body. Exercise restores your energy. If you're doing big things, you need your body to be healthy.

Raw. Eat raw food. If you want to go to the moon, only rocket fuel will do.

Rest. Rest well. Get good sleep. Many leaders do not get enough quality sleep. But if we do recharge the batteries, we'll be so much more effective.

Reflect. Actually take time to reflect. All too often we're so busy that we don't take time to just think—to do nothing else but think, pray, or meditate. If you want to have good mental health, take time out to reflect, if for no other reason than to make sure you're on the right track in your life.

Things will get difficult for everyone. But if you're maintaining healthy habits, you'll sail through them more easily and more quickly than those around you who are not doing so.

To Those Tempted to Quit

Confusion between *perfection* and *excellence* has defeated so many people who could've continued to do good work. We think we're supposed to achieve perfection, and when we don't—and we surely won't achieve it very often or for very long, if at all—we think we've failed. We may feel our perceived failure so intensely that we let it defeat us and cause us to drop out of the race.

Perfection is deadly, but excellence gives life. Perfection is like religion in the bad sense in which you cannot make a mistake. If you fail to achieve and maintain perfection, you are out. You are damned. You were obviously never "in" in the first place. This is a doctrine of death. Whereas with excellence, you can actually make mistakes. Now, it's not excellent to make a mistake, but it is excellent to learn from your mistakes.

Those who hold to the spirit of perfection are in bondage, and those who hold others to the standard of perfection are trying to put them in bondage. Perfection is useless. Excellence is where life is. A strong family is not perfect, but it is assuredly excellent.

Perfection is getting things done right on time but no earlier. Excellence is going overtime. If you can operate from a philosophy like that—going above and beyond—you'll be in a healthy place. A football team may not achieve perfection yet may maintain a high level of excellence. You don't have to win every game to win the championship, but you do have to maintain a winning spirit—especially when there are setbacks.

Healthy Self-Talk

We live in an age in which we are bombarded with competing messages trying to gain our attention. Sometimes advertisers and marketers use manipulative tricks in order to gain our attention. The idea is that if we can capture your thoughts and influence your heart, then we might just influence your consumer behavior as well.

What we're talking about here is *persuasion*.

We persuade ourselves all the time. Sometimes we persuade ourselves in positive ways and sometimes in negative ways. When the alarm goes off at five thirty in the morning and you have every intention to go exercise, you have to persuade yourself to actually get up and go do it. If it's late at night and you're feeling a bit peckish and there's that last slice of chocolate cake in the fridge, well, there's a certain seductive dance that takes place in your mind. Will we each persuade ourselves to do the healthy thing or yield to the seductive pull to do the other thing? The way to be persuasive and not seductive is not to seduce but rather to woo with wisdom.

That's a long way around to self-talk, but this is how we help people control their persuasive minds. We talk about priority, permission, and perspective.

If we want to build margin into our lives, we have to *prioritize*. We have to be well organized and make sure that our priorities are setting the course. How we prioritize for fitness is going to dictate whether we exercise or eat that chocolate cake. If we have prioritized fitness, the choice is clear cut.

We also have to recognize that giving in to temptation first requires our *permission*. As I said earlier, we give our permission for someone to offend us, because no one can offend you without your permission. We are complicit in the process. Who and what are we giving permission to? If we think about the mind being like a gate for thoughts, then we will see that we are the gatekeeper. What thoughts are we opening the gate to? What thoughts are we giving permission to? And what thoughts do we need to actually close out?

In order to do that, we need to maintain the right *perspective*. We gain the right perspective by answering these three questions: Who am I? Why am I here? And what am I worth? If you can answer those three questions in a healthy way, then in any situation you'll be able to woo yourself with wisdom to do the right thing.

That's how you control your thoughts and maintain healthy self-talk.

Pressing On through Trauma

I'm often asked how people should cope with trauma. I always respond by saying, "Wrong question."

If the person is a Christian, coping is the wrong focus. The Bible talks about transformation, not coping. The Christian life is not about putting up with trauma but about forgiving and forging ahead.

Health is about no longer being ruled by fear.

Trauma is actually a form of fear. The traumatized person's brain is tricking him or her always into thinking that the tragedy or the trauma is still taking place, and it causes anxiety and distress.

It's possible to use the latest research in psychology and neuroscience to help people learn the life skills to overcome all the *symptoms* associated with trauma: sleep disruptions, flashbacks, nightmares, and more. We can help bring relief and build resilience.

But unless a person also learns to reconcile his or her past, that person will never be able to actually get on with his or her future. To be truly free, a person also has to learn how to let go of the pain, bitterness, and resentment.

When we go around the world into war zones and disaster zones and sit down with groups of people who have come through our rehabilitation program, we always ask, "What was the most impactful part of the trauma rehabilitation process?" Hands down, the number one response will be something like "When I finally understood how to forgive."

When you give the gift of forgiveness, you discover that the gift is really intended for you.

Let me tell you just one story of a teenage girl who lived in northern Uganda. She was pregnant, and one day she and a couple of her girlfriends were out tilling the land with their hoes. A group of rebel soldiers came upon them and killed the other girls. But it was considered a bad omen to kill a pregnant girl. So instead of killing her, they just mutilated her horribly. They made one of their younger members take a knife to this precious girl's face. He cut off her nose. He cut off her ears. And he cut off her lips. But she was rescued and brought into World Vision's Children of War Rehabilitation Center in Gulu.

After a while this teenage girl recovered somewhat from her physical wounds. She was, of course, greatly disfigured. Her physical wounds ceased to bleed, but she had emotional wounds that continued to fester. Needless to say, she was reminded of the tragedy every time she looked in the mirror.

As it happened, it wasn't too much later that a child soldier showed up. He was a boy who had escaped from the rebel group and found refuge in the same World Vision rehabilitation center. The girl saw him and said, "That's him! That's the one who did this to me!"

Now, we'd been doing training with World Vision about the importance of reconciliation, so one of the facilitators said to her, "What would you like us to do?"

And she said, "You've been teaching me about forgiveness and reconciliation. Maybe I could give that a go."

Can you believe that kind of healing? That's not just over-coming or pressing on—that's letting go. That's the gift of forgiveness.

So the facilitators gathered all the kids together, and this young woman stood up and faced the boy who had mutilated her.

"You were the one who cut me and left me for dead," she said. "But from this day forward, I no longer hold this against you. I'm not going to be a captive to what you've done to me for the rest of my life. This is the day that I release you."

You have to understand that she wasn't excusing his behavior. There's no excuse for what he did. Even if he was forced to do it, he still had a choice. He could've chosen to be shot himself, but instead, he chose to preserve his life by ruining hers.

She went on to say, "This day I choose to let go of *my* pain and *my* hatred toward you."

You see, forgiveness has more to do with the gift giver than it has to do with the perpetrator.

The facilitators were blown away. But they thought it wouldn't last. How could one so young and so hurt be so able to forgive? They thought it's one thing to get up in front of a group of kids and say "I forgive you," but it's a whole other thing to actually live it out on a daily basis.

I like to say that forgiveness is similar to weight lifting. You can push the hurt and the bitterness away today, but tomorrow they come back. You have to push them away again, and again they come back. Every day you'll be reminded of what happened, and you'll have to keep pushing it away as a daily discipline. But through this process you build strength, and eventually you are able to put the weight down and let it go once and for all.

The facilitators decided to track this young lady over the weeks to come.

She eventually gave birth to her baby. Not long after, some of the facilitators walked around the corner and were shocked to see the perpetrator and the girl playing with the baby. They were laughing and taking photographs together.

That is the power of forgiveness. Friendship is by no means a prerequisite for forgiveness. However, the power of forgiveness is so great that it can even transform a mortal enemy into a friend. Forgiveness is not merely coping with hurt and pain; it's the springboard that launches you into a brand-new future.

I once heard Erin Rodgers, who was the contributor of chapter 1 in this book, talk about taking responsibility for her own opportunities. She told me about how, in her business, she hears many people complain that their managers haven't given them the tools or support they need to grow their business. She said the people who helped her get started in her company weren't always available to answer her questions or help her set goals. However, Erin had made the decision early on that her business, her success, and her opportunity were *her* responsibility. If someone didn't encourage her, it wasn't going to stop her. So what if others didn't do what they should've done? It wasn't an excuse for her to lie down and let her business die. If she needed something done, she wouldn't rest until she found a way to make it happen.

Your environment, your opportunity, is up to you. If you want to know whether your business, marriage, ministry, or plan is going to be successful, you can find out by checking how fully you have taken responsibility for your actions.

Our thoughts can keep us from greatness. We allow our fears of external forces or people to prevent us from doing what needs to be done to act on our opportunities. Entrepreneur Jen Jordan gives one example:

> Early on I had a really hard time reconciling the idea that I was making money off my friends. I had to make my peace with it. I had to get to the point where I could say, *It's OK, Jen. It's OK that you're getting paid to provide this service for people. You're taking time away from your family to equip people with the information you have that they don't have and are willing to pay to get. It's OK to get paid to do that. This is your job.* But if I hadn't gotten past that, I never would've become successful at this business.

Your life is up to you, and its success will be based largely on whether or not you take responsibility for it. That means that responsibility is an opportunity. You get to own it. You get to create it. You get to become whom and what you want to become. There is nothing holding you back. It doesn't matter if you didn't come from a wealthy family. It doesn't matter if you didn't receive an Ivy League education. It doesn't matter if you tried before and failed. It doesn't matter if you suffered abuse, hardship, and injustice.

Take it from someone who sees people come out of slavery: there are many people who have dealt with much worse than you and I will ever have to face, and they have succeeded. Their excuses would be much more powerful and convincing than ours, and they have pursued and achieved their impossible despite their circumstances. How? By taking responsibility.

They have owned their opportunity. They have bossed it. They have become it. They have seen it through. They have donned the attitude of a deliverer.

What are the external circumstances in your life that you are blaming for keeping you small and in the phase of intention only? Write them down.

Now, how are you going to take responsibility? What are you going to do differently? How are you going to change your language to show yourself and everyone around you that you are now responsible for your attitudes, behaviors, and actions?

Take up the reins of your own life. No one else is holding them, despite what you may have let yourself believe. If you want a different life, build it. The opportunity is right there in front of you. Your opportunity is your responsibility.

DISCUSSION QUESTIONS

1. What is *your* opportunity of responsibility? What are your areas of responsibility?

2. Is there a "because of" that you are allowing to be a barrier to your greatness? What have you given permission to stand between you and the life you want to lead?
3. Dr. Robi said that some people are hindered by the impact of trauma and others become better after their trauma than they were before. What makes the difference?

4

YOUR VIBE ATTRACTS
YOUR TRIBE

By this stage I hope you have asked questions of your frustration, innovated in your thinking about solutions, and accepted that responsibility is an opportunity. Look how powerful you are!

You've reached the point in the process where you're going to need a team. I know you're feeling unstoppable and ready to be unleashed on the world, but the biggest challenges are not solved alone. The reality is, if you are trying to do this alone, you will always reach your limit and limit your reach.

The Egyptian pyramids were not built by the pharaoh alone. Rome wasn't built in a day (or by any one leader toiling away by himself). No nation was built by any one person, no matter what the propaganda leaflets may say. Innovations and breakthroughs can come through individual effort, but no grand campaign is ever won by any hero or heroine working alone.

Michael Jordan, the legendary all-star basketball player, is credited with saying, "Talent wins games, but teamwork and intelligence win championships."[1]

Add this saying to your self-talk right now: I. Can't. Do. This. Alone.

I often say at Hope for Justice, "Fact: I cannot end slavery alone."

Pause there. Look at your vision. Look at what you are trying to achieve. And say it aloud: "I can't do this alone." Your goal may be building the biggest business empire. Say, "Fact: I can't do it alone." Your challenge may be to have the best marriage. "Fact: I can't do it alone."

I have found that many entrepreneurs, including so many working in the social justice space, have a white-knight complex. They think they have to do it alone. They think they're the ones who will do it best so it's easier to do it alone. And frankly many of us (at least at first) *want* to do it on our own. If someone else shares the work, then won't someone else get to share the glory?

Hey, no judgment here. We may have many reasons for doing the work we do, especially at the outset. But not even the most chivalrous knight on the whitest of horses can conquer these dragons alone. You want to end world hunger by yourself? Knock yourself out. You want to end corruption in certain governments all on your own? Go for it. But you'll quickly find that the problems are huge, and you're going to need a way to multiply your efforts.

Teamwork is one of the greatest tools that can empower you to be the best version of yourself. You can't do it alone.

Hope for Justice isn't operated by one person. And it isn't supported by just one person or even one organization. We are supported by thousands of individuals every month. We have tens of thousands of followers on social media. We are often featured on global news channels. We have been invited to brief President Donald Trump, and we brief parliaments across the world about modern slavery. We are working with some of the largest corporations in the world. Hope for Justice is the work of multitudes.

It is a movement, right?

But it wasn't always a movement. Even the greatest organizations or movements begin when people join together.

Entrepreneur Jordan Schrandt recommends having a core group, especially at first, and perhaps building from there:

> I have a small, tight inner circle. I've learned to keep my inner circle small because I think it creates so much more strength and unity in my life. Not everyone is supposed to be our best friend. Some people can just be friends, but they can't be trusted with all the inner workings of our lives. Since we're always changing and becoming better day by day, our inner circles have the chance to see *progress* in us rather than looking for a *perfection* that others might try to demand of us. That is such a key that I think many of my peers miss. They think they should trust their hearts and lives to anyone who comes along. I think it's better to surround yourself with the sort of people you'd like to have more of in your life.

There is a TED Talk that features one crazy guy in a field dancing to music in the background. There are people around him, but they are not dancing with him. They are watching him—some laughing, some jeering. But he doesn't care. He dances, completely carefree. And then something amazing happens. Someone joins him. Together they dance wildly. And then someone else joins, and then someone else, until the nearly entire crowd in that field is dancing without any regard for what those around them are thinking. They have caught the vision and they are full of joy.[2]

A decade ago, I was that guy. I was just dancing, and everyone else was thinking, *He is weird. Why is he booking an arena? What is he doing?* Suddenly someone else wanted to join and became our first supporter. Everyone else was watching us and thinking, *What are those two doing? Why are they dancing?* Another person thought, *Actually that looks like fun*, and he jumped in. Then more and more jumped in.

There have always been a few who say, "I will never join in. That looks weird." Then even the negative, cynical Eeyores can come to realize they are not part of the vibe and they are not part of the tribe. But they want to be part of the vibe and the tribe, so they jump in. And the rest of us shout, "Woo-hoo!"

No one really knows or cares who started it. It was never about the person who started it. Hope for Justice isn't about a man; it's about a movement. It's about the vibe and the tribe. People catch the vision that something must be done about modern slavery—and that something *can* be done—so they join in the dance.

When you create something that resonates with people, they will want to join you. Your efforts and your vision will attract folks to the cause, to the vibe. Like attracts like.

You need to be intentional about the vibe you are giving off as an organization and even as an individual leader. You don't do this by accident. I have known people who have completely changed their wardrobe because they realized, *Wow, what I am currently wearing is communicating a vibe that will not attract the people who will help this vision become a reality.* They changed their vibe to attract the right tribe.

Others might realize they are overly negative in their language and this will attract (and probably already has attracted) a very negative tribe. They might catch themselves and think, *Oh my gosh, my vibe is so negative. Why did I just say that?* In meetings, they might notice they are the ones saying, "No. No. Can't be done." And one day they may look around and realize the people around them are the negative people. They might not remember joining such a group, but maybe the insight comes that your vibe attracts your tribe.

Be strategic with your vibe. Be deliberate. The main thing to get from this chapter is this: you get to decide what your vibe is. Ultimately that will be what attracts your tribe.

What you sow you will reap.

You need a team to tackle the big goals you have set for yourself. Every team member needs to be dancing to the same music, so be intentional about your tribe.

Speaking of music …

Natalie Grant is a recording artist with seven Grammy nominations and multiple Gospel Music Association Dove Awards, including five for Female Vocalist of the Year. She's incredibly successful as a musician. But I know her best as my friend and fellow abolitionist. She's a wonderful human being who has built a career and used her platform to effect change for some of the most vulnerable people all over the world. Her journey toward success is a beautiful illustration of how your vibe attracts your tribe.

I always loved singing, and people told me I was talented. But as I was growing up in Seattle, in the days before *American Idol*, I didn't have any plans of becoming a professional singer.

I did have a sense that God wanted me to sing, but I had no desire to be famous. I just noticed that something happened every time I opened my mouth. There was a shift in the atmosphere, and people reacted to my voice, and I could sense that even as a child. I knew there was a special gifting on my life, and I knew I wanted to sing in the local church. But that's as far as I ever thought it would go. After high school I went to college to study elementary education, and I thought I would become a schoolteacher.

Twenty years later, I've released ten albums and have had a full-time career in music. It's been an incredible ride, but it hasn't been an easy one.

YOUR VIBE ATTRACTS YOUR TRIBE

Over the last two decades, I've seen lots of people come and go. I've seen bands and groups and soloists, and I've seen extremely impressive people with amazing talent. Sometimes songs shoot to the top of lists and win awards. But I've seen many artists go as quickly as they came.

The music business is a brutal industry. It will tear you apart. If people's priorities are wrong and they're wanting fame and success to fix something broken in their lives or if they're trying to do it in their own strength, they're not going to make it.

But if I had to pick one quality that marks someone who makes it through the music industry with his or her sanity and balance still intact, I'd have to choose the quality of humility.

I respect Christian musician Steven Curtis Chapman. He's been doing music for so long, he's won so many awards, and he's had great success. Yet if you were to sit and talk with Steven, you wouldn't walk away starstruck having been in his presence. You would walk away impressed by how simple and genuine he is. The man just oozes humility. When I look at the people who have stayed around for decades in this industry, a crucial quality I see they have in common is humility.

Where does humility come from? I don't think you can simply *decide* to be humble. The only people who can truly be humble, I've found, are those who know they don't have to prove anything to anyone.

I see a lot of people come to Nashville, Tennessee, because they are seeking fame and success. But in reality these people often have deeply rooted insecurities and believe that success will fill the void they feel. When we don't build the foundation of our identity on who Christ says we are, we can't understand true humility. When we know our identity lies in who God says we are, we don't have anything to prove. We don't have to try to look impressive. Instead, we can be at peace with ourselves, and humility becomes a natural reflection of that.

I think one of the biggest downfalls for young artists is entitle-ment. I see this all the time. Young musicians feel entitled to their dream just because they have one. They feel entitled to success because they think they can sing. They probably can't articulate it, but I suspect their entitlement thinking comes from a place of shame or the belief that they need to prove their worth. How it often comes across, however, is that they believe they deserve success just for showing up.

It's hard to have an attitude of humility when you think the world owes you. Entitlement is the antithesis of having a ser-vant's heart.

For me humility expresses itself as making sure the people on my team are always taken care of. As long as I think my needs or my comfort is more important than theirs, I've left the path of servanthood. Humility must express itself in all areas of our lives: in our jobs, in our marriages, in our friendships, and in our daily conversations. We have to lead with humility. We have to be willing to serve. We have to be willing to prefer others over ourselves.

If humility is at the forefront of everything we do, we are going to attract the right kind of tribe.

It really is true that your vibe attracts your tribe. We don't even realize that we're giving off a vibe, but it becomes visible when we start to look at our social groups. If we're giving off a negative vibe, the people who don't live in the world of negativity won't want to be around us. But if we're giving off a positive vibe, negative people won't feel comfortable gossiping when we're with them. Either way, we will attract the people who are moving to the same melody we are, and we will repel the people who aren't.

Be really conscious of what vibe you're giving off. What kind of people do you want to have around you? Give off *that* vibe, and they'll come.

Of course, the perfect example of servant leadership is Jesus. He had a call. He had a goal. He had a vision. He was so strong and certain yet so wise and kind. He didn't lord His lordship over anyone. He was humble and even meek. But *meek* doesn't mean "weak." Jesus was determined and deeply heroic. But He was always humble, and He always served others.

We all need a tribe. We can't do extraordinary things on our own. I think it's really important for anyone who is chasing a dream to be self-aware and to know his or her limitations. None of us are called to do everything. None of us are good at everything. It's impossible. Sometimes we don't know when it's time to delegate and hand off to someone else. Someone around you may be extremely good at and passionate about the very thing you hate. Why not empower that person to run with it?

When everyone on the team is doing what he or she is good at and when everything that needs to be done is handled by people who are enjoying what they do, the overall tribe will be satisfied. And when everyone is satisfied, great things are likely to happen.

I look not only to attract my tribe but also to *keep* my tribe. I don't want to put a great team together and know they'll be together for only a moment. I want longevity in every area of my life: in my music, in my ministry, in my friendships, in my work relationships, in my work with Hope for Justice, and in my family.

I have that now. I have people on my team and in my band who have been with me for a very long time. I've found that loyalty is a two-way street, and when I'm loyal to my tribe, they in turn are loyal to me. I want my team to be around for the long haul. I've found that loyalty, like humility, is one of the greatest keys to having longevity in this industry.

Building a Tribe on the Large Scale

It's important to attract a team that harmonizes well with you in the everyday rhythms of working together, traveling together, and doing business together. But it's also important to find like-minded people you can build alliances with on a larger scale.

I got into the world of modern slavery—and modern abolition—because of one episode of a TV show. Over fifteen years ago, I saw an episode of a crime drama in which girls were being sold as human slaves out of the back of a van in New York City. I had never heard of such a thing. Honestly I didn't believe it was true. I thought, *This is not happening. There are not kids being held in people's basements in New York. That's preposterous. The writers blew it this time.*

I was so upset about it that I actually got up and googled it. Part of me was thinking, *But wait. What if this is true?* Of course, I found out right away that it really was true.

It haunted me. It's bad enough to think it's happening on the other side of the world. But to think it's happening right here in the United States? What could I do with that knowledge? I couldn't unknow it. What do you do when you find out that the most innocent among you are being ravaged in the most horrific way? How can you go to bed at night and act as if you don't know that?

I didn't know what it was going to be, but I knew I had to do something about it.

My husband and I went to India and saw trafficking happening right before our eyes, and we were absolutely wrecked. When we came back, we started looking for an organization we could work with, but we found that there weren't many of them in 2004. There weren't a lot of people talking about trafficking at that time. I'd never heard about it before that TV show, and most people I knew had never heard about it.

So we started our own organization, basically because we didn't know what else to do. We began by raising money to fund the abolitionist organization in India. We didn't know what we were doing, but we became an organization and funded projects in India, and the organization started taking off. We soon began attracting a tribe of people who wanted to join in the work.

It then became apparent that the organization had the potential to become something much larger than I knew how to handle. It was growing, but I recognized that while I was great at speaking about it from my platform and raising awareness of the issue, I wasn't equipped to be the one to take the work across the earth.

That's when I met Ben Cooley, head of Hope for Justice. He absolutely was the guy God had called and equipped to take the work far and wide. Our organizations were so like-minded, but our gifts were so different. It was with great joy and relief that we merged our organizations. On a very large scale, we were each able to do what we had been called to do while allowing others to do the parts they had been called to do, and it all got done.

At the level of your local team, your vibe attracts your tribe. But keep an eye out, too, for how your vibe might attract other organizations and allow you to create massive synergy and multiply your power in the work you're all called into.

When There's a Bad Fit

Sometimes, despite our best efforts to attract the right people for our tribe, we bring on someone who just isn't a good fit. It doesn't mean there is anything wrong with that person. It may just mean that person would be happier and more effective somewhere else.

But this is always a hard situation for me. I'm a fixer by nature and I can be a loyalist to a fault. I have probably allowed people to stay on the team for way longer than they ever should have been there.

In one situation I felt certain that God was telling me a chapter was closing on a working relationship with a teammate. I knew it was going to be painful, but I also knew I had to press through and do the hard thing of releasing this person. When it's time for somebody to move off your team, as a leader you have to remember that it is your responsibility to walk it out to the end. I've also learned that it's possible to do it in a way that's redemptive and beautiful. But despite your best efforts, that person might still be devastated at the decision.

At that point you have to come to terms with the fact that you're not responsible for how that person responds. You're responsible only for how you handle yourself and how you deliver your words. In my case of releasing someone from the team, the person actually ended up being much happier in a new setting and has flourished in a beautiful way. But in that moment it was extremely hard to have that conversation.

When I'm looking to add members to my tribe, I always seek like-minded people. As a Christian, being in tune with the Holy Spirit helps me discern who may be a good fit for the team from a personality, skill, and spiritual standpoint. When I'm in tune with the Spirit, I also don't have to work so hard to exude a certain vibe. I know He flows through me and that in itself will attract a tribe of like-minded people.

When Things Get Difficult

I did not have overnight success. At one point, though, I thought I would.

I moved to Nashville to pursue a career in music, and I got a record deal really quickly. It seemed as if everything was falling into place. I thought, *The Lord's anointing is on my voice and He has a plan. I'm now going to Nashville and I have a record deal.* It felt like the scenario every aspiring musician hopes for.

I recorded my first album, and the record label released my very first single. In the record business, especially back then, the number of albums sold in the first week is crucial. That first week's number, combined with the number of album preorders, determined how many marketing dollars were going to be allocated to push the record.

There I was, living the dream, with my single on the radio and my first album on sale.

And in that first week, my record company went out of business.

I remember thinking, *No, that can't be. It can't be closing down, because my first album and my first single just came out! This is not at all the way my story is supposed to play out!*

Not long after, I got a second record deal with another company. I made my second album and released another single. But not long after that second album released, that record company also closed.

I thought, *What is it about me?* Like, watch out, people—Natalie Grant shuts down record labels!

That was definitely my low point.

When the first record label closed, I thought, *Well, I guess that's just a setback.* I'm an optimist, so I rolled with it. But when the second one closed in the same way, it was devastating to me.

It made me examine something I'd always believed. Something that, it turns out, was really untrue and harmful.

Growing up, I had an understanding that the will of God was a huge mystical thing. I thought that if I took one wrong step to the right or to the left, I might be out of the will of God. When those record labels went out of business, I thought, *Wait. How could I have missed the will of God so badly? I thought I'd heard His voice. I thought this career in music was God's will for me.*

At that point it would have been really easy for me to quit. It would have been really easy to move back to Seattle and say, "OK, I tried it. Obviously being a professional singer wasn't God's will for my life. I'm going to move home and become a schoolteacher."

But I'm so glad I didn't. Because I can now look back and say that the closing of those record labels was the greatest thing that ever happened to me. Processing that confusion and pain is what taught me that life isn't about a destination or a chart position or a number one record. And I learned that's also not what God's will is about. God's will is all about the posture of my heart before Him.

It was such a freeing moment for me when I realized that God's will is for us to do all the things that He makes very clear in His Word. These important instructions: "Love the Lord your God with all your heart ... soul and ... mind" (Matt. 22:37); "Love your neighbor as yourself" (Matt. 22:39); "Pray continually" (1 Thess. 5:17); "Rejoice ... always" (Phil. 4:4); and "Give thanks in all circumstances" (1 Thess. 5:18).

These are the things God requires of us. Are you loving your neighbors, serving your community, giving thanks, and putting Him above all else? If you do the big things you know He wants you to do, then *you* get to pick what you want to do with your life. You don't have to worry about whether God's will is for you to take a certain job, move to a certain city, or pick up a certain hobby. You don't have to fear that you'll miss God's one and only "right" choice for you.

As long as you're doing the things God instructs us to do in His Word, then you get to do what you want. Psalm 37:4 says,

"Delight yourself in the LORD; and He will give you the desires of your heart" (NASB). So pick a career you want. Enjoy a pastime you love. Being in God's will isn't a magic potion, and it isn't about getting every decision right. It's about having your heart right. Because when your heart is right before Him, you'll make decisions that will be in line with His heart and His will for your life.

People ask me all the time, "How are you still doing this twenty years later?" I say, "Number one: Nobody can thwart God's plans for our lives. He has a purpose for each one of us, and He will work every piece of our lives together for our good. Our job is to trust Him and be obedient to His Word. And number two: I never would have chosen the hardships I've endured, but those hardships are what has helped build my faith and my character, and that's what's sustained me. I wouldn't want it any other way."

To Those Tempted to Quit

Sometimes people think about throwing in the towel because they realize they're doing something for the wrong reasons.

As Christians we have to make sure that our "want to" is rooted in Christ. There's a difference between working hard to finish the course and *striving* through purely human perseverance. There's a fine line between saying "This is what I'm going to do, and I'm never going to give up, because it's what God's called me to do" and saying "I'm never going to give up and I won't be denied." Human perseverance alone isn't enough. People in the music industry get this twisted all the time. There's an attitude of following God's call and then there's simply wanting to be successful.

Every person who has a dream has to get really honest and take inventory of his or her heart to determine what that dream is rooted in, and why he or she is so desperate for it to become a reality.

Even now, after twenty years, as I'm working on a brand-new record, I'm constantly asking myself, *Are you making this particular musical choice because you want the songs of Christ or because you think this song will be a hit on the radio?*

To the person thinking of quitting, I'd say to take the temperature of your heart and evaluate your motives. If you find that your motives are as they should be but you're still thinking of quitting, I'd then recommend looking for a place to serve where no one knows who you are. Find a local church or some other place to serve where you're working with people who know you only by your first name. Become that person who cleans the toilets or washes out the bus after the youth ski trip. Get in a position of servanthood. Serving just because you love God, not because you want recognition, is a great way to reset your perspective on your situation.

Step back and gain perspective. Sometimes we want to quit because we're frustrated or overwhelmed or just can't see past ourselves. My work with Hope for Justice is work that really matters. We are literally setting people free. When I get uptight about something that's not going as I had planned in my music career or I have a problem with my car or I'm frustrated in traffic, all I have to do is think about these children in bondage, and suddenly

I have a true perspective on the blessings in my life. In those moments I have the choice to practice gratitude and allow my perspective to change.

I recommend taking the time to step back and try to observe your situation from an outside perspective. Where do your problems and frustrations fit in the grand scheme of things? It may be that you find your desire to keep going—or you may even realize in that moment that you're ready to change directions.

If you do those things mentioned above (examining your motives, serving, and gaining an outside perspective) for a season and still want to quit, then it's probably OK to move on to the next chapter. Making a decision in this way will mean that your desire to make a change comes from the right motives, a humble heart, and a sweeping view of life.

In addition to what Natalie has said, there are four principles I want you to know about building a tribe.

First, what you sow you will reap. Make sure you are deliberate about what you sow.

Second, people like to be invited. Unfortunately, if you want to build a tribe, people often won't come to you—you have to invite them. But that's OK, because people like to be invited. Keep that in mind when you are developing that concept or starting that business. I can't tell you the number of people who have said to me, "I would have helped you, but you never asked."

There is a principle that says, "You do not have because you do not ask" (James 4:2). So start asking! You may not have that person in your tribe simply because you haven't asked him or her to join you.

I love telling the stories of people who joined Hope for Justice after leading multimillion-dollar businesses … because I asked them to. They were waiting to be invited, and they were pleased when I did so.

Third, people like to be thanked. I cannot emphasize this point enough!

Pastor John Siebeling and his team have a multicampus church organization in Memphis, Tennessee. John's story is an amazing testament to perseverance and small beginnings that lead to great growth. But one of the other things Pastor John is known for is celebrating what other people are doing and honoring those who might be overlooked. He knows people like to be thanked. In nearly every church service, he brings someone onstage to be interviewed or celebrated, and this attracts a humble and others-focused tribe.

Here's a bit from Pastor John:

> Honor is what I call a gateway virtue because it opens the door for good to flow into our lives. If I honor and respect you, it's going to open up things. Jesus said there's a reward that comes when you give a drink of water to someone who is thirsty. He said that if we do this to "these little ones" among us, it's as if we're doing it for Him [see Matt. 10:40–42].

When Jesus talked about "these little ones," I think He meant all the people we tend to ignore or overlook: the people who serve you at a restaurant, the people who work for you, the people we probably don't think about honoring. In our culture, of course we give honor to those who are above us. But in God's kingdom, we are also to honor our peers and those we oversee. I've heard it said that God gives honor up, down, and all around, and we should do the same.

When we show our thankfulness to those around us, I think it not only opens doors between people but also pleases God.

Fourth, if you think you are currently thanking people enough, double it. And then double it again. A tribe *loves* to be encouraged. There is something about human nature that loves to be thanked. People want to be appreciated.

When was the last time you gave time, money, or energy to something and then felt unappreciated for doing so? Did you do it again? Probably not. Because you want to go where you are thanked.

Guess what? So does your tribe. They want it so badly they will leave you if you don't celebrate, thank, and appreciate them. Your tribe will go where it is celebrated. You might be able to *attract* a tribe, but if you want to *keep* a tribe, you need to thank people … a lot.

Maybe you're thinking, *Yes, I run a business, and people keep leaving. Why is that?* Maybe it's because you were not thanking them enough. Maybe you didn't celebrate people. Maybe you have not adopted principles of appreciation.

The good news is that you have opportunity in the responsibility to change how you do things. Water a dying plant and watch it spring back to life.

One of our staff members from Canada recently joined the UK team. Her parents flew in to see her and the office (and, I suspect, whether or not we were a legitimate outfit!). I decided to thank them. Not just to thank the employee but to thank her family. Suddenly our staff member smiled so widely and stood so proudly you would've thought she was nine feet tall. Of course, her parents were overjoyed. Here was a place where people would get appreciated and *seen* for what they did.

Build appreciation into your organization's culture. Every week our team members do "Friday Shout-Outs," where they celebrate a colleague for some work that person has done or something that has contributed to the team that week. This is not a quick win or a one-time note of appreciation. This is part of our culture. It is now part of who I am.

If you want to sustain a tribe, you must thank them often.

DISCUSSION QUESTIONS

1. If you were to apply the idea "I can't do this alone," what changes would you make?

2. What sorts of people do you wish to attract to your endeavor, and what vibe could you exhibit to attract them? How might you make those qualities part of the fabric of your organization or project?

3. Who in your world can help you make your vision a reality?

WHAT YOU TOLERATE YOU'LL NEVER CHANGE

"What you tolerate you will never change" is by far one of the most profound phrases we use within Hope for Justice. This idea is challenging to anyone at any stage of life, no matter his or her experiences, achievements, or background.

When I want to evaluate the health of my team or my leadership (or anything else), I ask myself, *What am I tolerating that should change?* The problem is that I hate confrontation. I have an innate insecurity that makes me a conflict avoider. When I know a situation could be better and change would help us get further and faster ... I tend to avoid addressing the issue as long as I can.

In the same way that we have always thought of frustration as a bad thing, we often see conflict as negative too. Yet, as you've probably already guessed, conflict can be our friend.

Almost all the successful leaders I have ever met have also tried to hide from conflict. They put it aside at some point, hoping it would go away. But something in them changed and caused them to confront conflict, which was a turning point in their careers. They had to force themselves to face conflict. Because, unfortunately, conflict is not going away.

When you pursue your impossible or try to make changes in the world, you will face conflict. And why would we expect anything less? It's because of our frustration with how things are that we got involved in the first place, right? We have in our minds' eyes possibilities that are *in conflict with* reality, and we've decided to go up against it. In a rapidly changing world, in a continually shifting environment, in a growing family, in an evolving economy, there will always be new challenges.

Maybe you're in conflict with people who lead in a way that you wouldn't lead. Maybe your work is in direct conflict with people and systems that very much prefer the status quo. Maybe there are attitudes within your tribe that are not your vibe and you want that to change.

You have to learn the art of conflict resolution.

In order to go to new heights and continue the movement toward your vision, you need to face and resolve conflict. Failing to address the issues that are hindering your movement will stop your momentum.

Sometimes differences can emerge in your leadership team even years down the road. Subtle differences in vision or agenda can cause a strain that could ultimately split the organization down the middle.

As the leader you may not want to address that conflict, especially if it's with someone who's been laboring beside you since the early days. But avoiding it will only make things worse. You may lose other good people because of the growing tension, and you risk even more disastrous outcomes the longer you wait.

Highly successful entrepreneur Jen Jordan learned how important it was for her success to find a way to overcome her reluctance to tackle conflict:

> Early on, probably the biggest challenge was knowing that people were not always going to be pleased with me. I tell my husband often, "Sorry, hon. I'm just a big ball of disappointment. Welcome to being married to me." It's true in business too. I'm going to disappoint people every day. I'm going to fail. I'm going to drop the ball. I'm going to forget something. I'm going to say something in a way that I didn't mean to be offensive but that offends you.
>
> First I had to learn how to humble myself and apologize when I am wrong. But immediately after that I had to learn how to call someone out when he or she is wrong. That might have been even harder. It was very uncomfortable for me. It's still not something I love. I'm just OK with it now.
>
> That's why you need to go to personal-growth seminars or read books on this topic. Dealing with people and being in conflict with them sometimes is part of any business. It's part of life. I know I

couldn't have grown to the next level of leadership without learning how to do that.

The cool thing is that addressing conflict blessed my marriage too! Learning how to humble myself and also to call people to a high standard has overflowed into all my other relationships. If you ignore certain issues, they'll never improve.

History is littered with examples of people ignoring negative situations because they didn't want to face the conflict, and avoiding confrontation caused division in families, companies, churches, and countries.

Hey, it's OK. We've all been there. We've all waited too long. Myself included. I waited too long on at least one occasion, hoping the difficult conversation would never come up. But it only made things worse. We've all tried to stick it out and hope the situation resolves itself. But I want you to acknowledge this principle: what you tolerate you will never change. I had to come to terms with it too.

My guess is that you are not OK with the fact that your organization is dividing, that your marriage is splitting, that your children are walking away, or that some great injustice is being allowed to continue. Who would be? If you're not OK with it, you can't let it endure. If you let it endure, you're tolerating it, so it will never change.

Guess what? Even if you try to avoid conflict, you can't. More conflict will come. I can promise that.

You will never *want* to have that difficult conversation. But when you finally decide to have it, it's a good idea to rehearse what you want to say. Practice it a few times in front of a mirror. Decide where, when, and how you want to have the conversation to resolve this conflict. Decide what resolution will look like in this scenario. What behavior do you want to change? Think about your endgame.

This is not about going in for a fight. This is about finding a positive resolution.

Sometimes the situation can be resolved and nothing else needs to change. Some conflict creates more rounded, more motivated individuals, and your team is stronger for it. Other times the situation can't be resolved and you have to make a larger change. In the end, if a resolution can't be found, the parting of ways will be the better result for all parties.

If you know there is a situation you need to address, if you know someone in your tribe is not dancing to your vibe, muster up your courage and have the conversation. What you tolerate you will never change. If you want something to change, you're going to have to stop tolerating the bad situation.

My friend David Kinnaman, whom I've known for many years, is a perfect example of mobilizing his efforts to bring about a change, though it was difficult because he had great respect for the person who had founded the organization.

One side note: I'll always be indebted to David for how he has spoken into my life. I'll never forget sitting across the table with him at a restaurant. There were other people all around, but after I shared something, David—with laser focus—spoke so clearly into my life. I felt like a little boy when this man of great stature spoke directly into my heart. We all need people like David to speak truth into our lives and to speak truth into our storms and into our characters.

Now for David's story about the change he brought about in a well-known organization.

In 1984 a gentleman named George Barna started a social research company that would be similar to the Gallup Poll company but from a Christian perspective. I joined the company as a twenty-one-year-old intern in the late 1990s, and I've been there ever since. In 2009 I purchased the company from George, and now I am owner and president of Barna Group.

Our work involves social research in which we interview hundreds of thousands of people in the United States and across the world as we try to understand people's perspectives and values. We use that market research to inform leaders and help them make better decisions about what they're up to and how to make the best of their opportunities. A lot of our work focuses on how faith and religion are powerful motivators in people's lives.

Recently we did a presentation for Sony Pictures in Los Angeles about how faith and religion drive moviegoing decisions. It was funny how uncomfortable the Sony executives were during our presentation. It's kind of an unspoken rule that religion is a taboo topic among executives in mainstream companies. Boardroom conversations are mostly about profits and marketing demographics. In most boardrooms across the country, you can talk about any sort of topic, even political topics, but you can't talk about religion.

That's part of what makes our company so valuable
They know religion is out there as a force behind co.
behavior, but because they're not allowed to talk about it, th
never able to think clearly about people of faith and what
want. That's a good example of the idea that what you toler
you'll never change. But some brave secular companies decic
not to tolerate their ignorance about faith anymore, so they cal
us to come talk to them about it.

Our company goes into movie studios, businesses, churches,
nonprofits, and corporations, and we help them understand how
central faith is to people's lives. We regularly surprise people in
our presentations with the fact that everyone is powerfully motivated by religion and spirituality, even people who don't have
a faith. Even if they are atheist or agnostic, religious elements
shape how they make consumer decisions, how they think about
their lives and identities, what is important to them, how they
think about generosity, and more.

WHAT YOU TOLERATE YOU'LL NEVER CHANGE

Sometimes our research at Barna reveals a troubling trend in th
culture, and we're not really set up to change those things. So
show the information to leaders and churches and the public
hope they'll rise up and change those things.

It's frustrating, because I firmly believe that what you
erate you'll never change. If we're only pointing out trend
we tolerating something that really needs to change? I de
a considerable amount of prayer to the hope that our r

will be the *agent* of change, the provocative "wow" moment that causes people to wake up and take action.

We did a study a couple of years ago in which we asked people about the way they make decisions. We were most interested in how people formed their identities and where they got their ideas for how they could improve as individuals.

As researchers we're very careful not to influence how people respond, but we're also humans with brains, so we have expectations about how most people are likely to answer certain questions. Since the US has a high percentage of people who call themselves Christian,[1] I personally thought most respondents would say they get their identity from God and their ideas about improvement from the Bible. Boy, was I surprised.

What we found was that *91 percent* of adults think that the best way to "find yourself" is to look within yourself.[2] I had heard recently that some younger leaders are realizing that the self-centered sort of entitlement approach to life doesn't make sense, so I expected to see a turn from that inward focus. That's why I found it really fascinating—and somewhat disquieting—that a majority of adults think the best way to find themselves is to look within themselves. Can I take off my neutral researcher's hat for a minute and say that is really a crazy idea? Apparently this sort of morality of self-fulfillment has become the new moral structure.

What can we do to stop tolerating that so it does actually change?

We also found that 89 percent of adults say it's wrong to criticize someone else's life choices.[3] The preferred response is

to say you can believe whatever you want, and the expectation is that those beliefs and choices won't negatively affect society.

For example, a majority of people believe we shouldn't criticize someone for viewing pornography. Somehow they think tolerating the viewing of pornography doesn't affect society. What about the women and men—and children—who are victimized and exploited for pornographic purposes? How is the porn industry *not* negatively affecting society? What if it was your daughter or son being exploited? What if your family was torn apart by pornography? How does any of that not negatively affect society? Yet we're not supposed to criticize anyone's life choices. Pornography is now morally acceptable in the minds of a vast majority of adults. People use this thinking to justify their own actions, but they do not understand the impact it has on society. Listen. What we tolerate we'll never change.

A Transition of Power

George Barna is one of my mentors. I deeply admire and respect him, both as a person and for what he accomplished with Barna Group. When I began to think, over the course of several years, that I might want to steer the company in a different direction—or that I might even be able to do some things better than him—it was daunting.

This wasn't a case of tolerating something bad, not at all. Yet it was a case of me wanting to make a change ... which meant I couldn't keep things going as they had. I began to have a different sense of where the company could go.

By this point I had risen in the ranks and was president of the company. George had talked openly and often about how he wanted to eventually hand the keys over to me, and I was daring to think what I might do differently if I were at the helm.

George had been my friend, my mentor, founder of the company, and he was an amazing guy and leader, so it was hard to acknowledge in my mind that I thought I could do better. I really respect him, and he'd done a fantastic job for twenty-five years running the company, but I believe God puts in young leaders the desire to challenge the process.

Thinking you can do better can be a good thing or a bad thing. The question is, What do you do with that? Are you going to get cynical and corrosive to the organization's culture? Are you going to complain and talk about things in a way that doesn't produce beneficial outcomes for the company? It's important to remain loyal to the current vision as long as it's the one the company is going with. But you can plan and dream and explore as you wait and support the current leadership.

Transitions can be difficult. And in my case, things got a little tricky. George left Barna to head up another company that he was very excited about. He made me the official boss of Barna Group, and he moved to a new opportunity. He gave me the car keys, so to speak, and went out to pursue his new challenge. That was fantastic, and I began implementing the things I'd been planning to do.

But George's new venture didn't work out the way he had planned, and after a time he came back to Barna Group. I had transitioned into my role, and I was taking the company in new directions, but George went back into the old mode. I still remember the day he came into my office with this memo of things he wanted us to do. When he'd been in charge and I'd been his president, I'd always loved hearing his new ideas. But now things were different, yet he didn't see them as different. It was as if he wanted the car keys back.

This was a situation that, if I tolerated it even once, might never change. So I talked to him about it, and he agreed. He started talking about wanting to sell the company. It was still his, of course, and I told him I would stay on with the new owners so he could get top value in the sale.

At the same time, I saw this as my opportunity to do what I really wanted to do.

"George," I said, "you know I don't come from wealth, so we need to figure out a creative way to do this. But I want to buy Barna Group. I'm going to request that you and Nancy"—his wife and co-owner of the business—"talk about whether you'd like me to buy it or if you want to find bidders. I don't want to compete against myself. So please first decide if you want me to own it. And if you do, then let's get creative with financing and make it happen."

I left it with him and Nancy to talk and pray about. That was a big risk for me. I could've tried to win the bidding war and buy the company outright. But I wanted George and Nancy to prefer me as the new owner. I had to give up my dream of owning the business. I put the choice in George's hands, refusing to take it in mine, and let him decide. And what if they wanted to go with the full bidding route? I'd already promised I'd stay with the company no matter what, but I would've been heartbroken to not own it.

Happily they decided they wanted me to buy them out, and I did. Even though it was a risk for me to let them choose, I think it resulted in a better outcome than if I had just come in and said, "Hey, I want to buy this business, and these are the terms." In any negotiation you have to think in terms of win-win. How can everyone around the table win?

When Things Get Difficult

It's now been about a decade since I purchased the company. I find it funny that before the succession I would say to myself, *If I owned the company, I would do things a lot differently*, but now, sitting in that seat, I'm beginning to understand why George did what he did. I may still choose a different path, but now I recognize the considerations he had as the leader and owner, trying to keep things from getting overly complicated.

I struggled with trying to compete with the way things were done before I was the owner. There might be new people around me in the office, but there were some longtimers who very clearly remembered—and liked—the way things had been when I was just an intern.

The second-generation leader is always under the specter of the old regime. Sometimes I find myself wanting to do things differently not because they were bad but just so I can feel as if I'm the one driving the ship! Sometimes the worst thing about my leadership is that I'm trying to do things differently to escape the shadows I think I live under.

If you're an aspiring leader, it's important to keep your heart right. In your position it's really easy to see the gap between your vision and the vision of the CEO. Write down those things. Keep them in your mind. Start making a list of things you would do differently. But also bear in mind that there may be reasons you don't yet understand for why things are being done that way. There may be considerations you have no clue about. Stay humble. Practice healthy methods of challenging the process. Do so in a constructive way that leads everyone to a win-win.

But I know that sometimes this is difficult. Before the succession I had to keep my heart right. I had to learn the hard truth that no good can come out of my angry complaints or the arrogance that I could do a better job. It's better to spend your energy helping the leader achieve his or her goals. Your time will come.

Our Lowest Point

How well I remember that moment when I was the new owner and the first payroll was coming up. The bills started coming in, and I realized, *This is on me now. This is now 100 percent my responsibility.* It was a sobering thought.

It got worse about eleven months after I'd bought Barna Group when we discovered that one of my people had been stealing money from the business. It was 2009, the economy was terrible, and we had only four or five people working in the office. We were scratching and clawing to make every dollar as it was. And then to realize that one of my trusted people had stolen hundreds of thousands of dollars from the business over the course of the year ...

In that first year I had mostly been using muscle memory to run the company the way it had already been running. I was finding my sea legs, and it was tough to make ends meet. But it got a whole lot tougher to make ends meet—and to keep my chin up—when somebody stole money from my company.

I remember thinking this was my *Braveheart* moment. I had a feeling in the pit of my stomach that this betrayal was not going to end us. I remember thinking, *This is my company, and I'm going to save it. We're going to find a way. I'm going to rally all the people around us, and I may have to put my own money on the table, but this is not going to end us.* So we got on the phone with various vendors and some of our investors and said, "Look. Here's the situation. We're heartbroken. But we have a plan to make this right."

That was definitely one of our defining moments. We realized that we may come up against the worst of human nature, but it called something out of us too. It became so personal to me then, and I was willing to put my own bank account on the line to make it work. I rallied our team and tried to use my words to persuade people that it was going to work out right. I remember telling people, "All right, yes, this isn't the best financial picture right now, but let's believe in the vision of where we're going." I discovered things about myself that I never would've known if I'd not gone through that tough season.

I've realized that leadership is not easy and that it costs something. Nothing extraordinary happens in this world without a cost, and sometimes the people who pay most are the leaders.

I've also learned through it all that people think leadership is a straight line to glory. People see leaders having success in business or the arts, and they think, **Wow, his or her life must be so amazing.** They see someone on TV or in the news or leading a big organization, and things seem to be working out for that person. It's easy to envy him or her. But it's never that simple.

We think leadership is a straight line, but really it is a circuitous thing with all kinds of ups and downs. And really, the ups and downs happen *at the same time*. We can gain a new client and have someone quit the business on the same day. We can have wonderful success and acclaim in the morning, and in the afternoon a family member might get a devastating health diagnosis. It's a challenge to keep your balance and keep moving forward.

My dad has been a lifelong pastor. For thirty years in a row, he kept growing his church in Phoenix, Arizona. It got bigger and bigger until it was one of the biggest megachurches in Phoenix, with about five thousand weekly attenders. During that time he felt as if he was an amazing leader who had done many things right.

But then the church started to decline. Year after year the number of attenders—and the money that came in—dropped. That sent my father into a period of deep soul-searching. Because if his great leadership had led to the growth, was the decline to be pinned on him because somehow he'd become a poor leader?

He finally realized his identity had been tied to the growth of the church—which meant it was also tied to its decline. But what he discovered was that he hadn't really been the cause of its growth. It wasn't about his leadership or charisma or business decisions. It wasn't about him at all. He realized that all the good years and all the good things that had happened weren't his doing. Something special had happened, but it wasn't about him.

That was hard for him to admit, but it was also what saved him. Because he immediately realized that the decline wasn't his fault either.

To Those Tempted to Quit

Leadership is keeping your balance and making progress even against the headwinds of life. It's not about your personality or your skills, and if you want to survive as a leader, you can't connect your organization's success with your identity. That's a trap.

So what do you do? You stay faithful. You do your best. You wake up and make the right choice. You decide to maintain the right attitude about your boss, your employees, and your situation. You choose hope and joy. You try to influence people in a positive way every day. Despite the setbacks you pick yourself up and choose to be positive instead of giving up. That's what makes great leaders. It's what makes great entrepreneurs, great moms and dads, and great people.

There are plenty of reasons any of us would choose to give up, given the sometimes-overwhelming nature of life, finances, illness, human nature, and business. But those hardships are what cause us to learn what's really in us. If we quit, we miss the chance to discover what we're capable of.

However, some of your projects or programs or even your business may not work out. Maybe you need to readjust, and maybe that looks like quitting on a particular direction. What matters is what you take from the experience.

We had a huge setback one time after we had invested tons of money and energy and a lot of my personal influence in a product that didn't take off. I was devastated when it didn't work out in the ways we had expected. We had thought a new series of products would dominate certain publishing categories, but it didn't happen at all the way we had imagined.

One of our advisers came to me and said, "Listen. Let's not waste a good failure. Let's learn from this. Several things worked well in this. Let's make a list of everything that worked and all the things that didn't. Let's take stock of what we learned as a company and what you learned as a leader."

It was fantastic advice, and we did what he suggested. Many of the programs and processes our company uses now are things we learned from that massive failure. Our healthy response to that failure propelled us to new heights of success later. We built on and started doing more of the things that worked. We do less of the things that didn't work.

Failure is a lesson. That's how you have to see it.

What you tolerate you'll never change. If we had simply cried in our soup over that failure and gone back to work the next day without learning from what had gone right and what had gone wrong, we never would've been able to have the success we enjoy today.

Sometimes the problem you are tolerating is not caused by someone else or by something external. Sometimes the problem you are tolerating is something that needs to change in you.

For too long I tolerated my inability to say no. I think this is a good example for many type A leaders. They are high achievers who always want to say yes. But Steve Jobs once said, "People think focus means saying yes to the thing you've got to focus on. But that's not what it means at all. It means saying no to the hundred other good ideas that there are."[4]

My yes is often said out of insecurity and FOMO (fear of missing out). If I say no to something or someone, I may miss out. But there is so much power in your no. Saying no could give you an opportunity for a better yes. It may seem as if you're saying no to a great opportunity, but it means that later you can give your yes to an even greater opportunity.

Many high achievers pack their schedules. For them busyness becomes a medal of honor. But for the best leaders, busyness is not the goal. *Health* is the goal. Healthy things grow. I have therefore begun saying no. No, I don't need to be in every meeting. No, I don't need to write that report. No, I don't need to answer every email. No, I don't need to oversee human resources. No, I don't need to control all my social media.

A leader's *no* for him- or herself is a *go* for someone else. My no is an opportunity to empower someone who has better skill, better experience, and greater capacity to do that thing.

If you're attempting big things, your business or movement cannot be limited to one person. You can't do this alone. Don't be the bottleneck that keeps your goal out of reach.

What are you saying yes to right now that you should be saying no to? What are you tolerating that you really do need to change? Have the difficult conversations so you can accelerate yourself and your team toward your goal.

DISCUSSION QUESTIONS

1. Name one thing you're tolerating that you should really change. What will your next steps be?
2. If you decide to quit your endeavor, what things have you learned or done well that you could apply to future projects?
3. What do you need to say no to in order for someone else to go for it?

CELEBRATE WHAT YOU WANT TO REPLICATE

When you work in difficult environments and you and your team see the worst of humanity, you learn that celebration is vitally important. Squaring off against human evil is not a situation in which you always go from victory to victory. Sometimes the wrong side wins a round. So you must celebrate your achievements and the difference you are making.

The art of celebration is one of the most powerful tools you can develop as a leader.

Parenting books often instruct parents to celebrate the good behavior of their children, because this reinforces the way they act and encourages them to repeat that behavior in the future.

Celebrate what you want to replicate.

Celebration reinforces culture. Early on in Hope for Justice, I realized we had a diluted, diverse, and divided culture within the organization. There were behaviors and attitudes I wanted us all to share, but I wasn't seeing them as much as I liked. So we used celebration to reinforce our vision and our values.

At first we did this by opening a bottle of champagne every time a victim was rescued from slavery through our efforts. We'd write the victim's name on the bottle and toast to our win against evil. That was a great morale booster, as you can imagine. And it worked very well—right up until we had seventy rescues in one day. That might have been a bit too much celebration! We thought maybe we needed a different approach.

The technique you use to celebrate your team doesn't really matter, as long as it encourages your group's core values and is the kind of thing you want to see more of in the future. Our friends at Christians Against Poverty play a harmonica every time someone becomes debt-free, and they sound a bell every time a client becomes free from addiction. There are different ways of celebrating, and you have to find the right one to fit your culture.

Entrepreneur Jordan Schrandt recognizes the power of encouraging the team and celebrating what you want to replicate:

> Disappointments can always turn into opportunities. A closed door leaves a ton of "What's next?" options. In that situation see alternatives that are amazing instead of doors that are closed. Mind-set is everything. Keep things positive; look for the good. Count your blessings, love the people who need you, and be kind.
>
> It starts with me staying motivated myself … and then getting buy-in from others! If I'm

motivated and creating energy and momentum, it's no fun if it's just me, so bringing people into that energy and momentum is the best thing ever. And it keeps everyone moving forward and motivated.

Smile. Dream. Cast your vision. Run! People will follow suit.

WHY CELEBRATION MATTERS

There are three reasons celebration matters for leaders.

First, celebration is vision in bite-size. This is particularly important when your vision is something large and seemingly unrealistic—or even impossible! Celebration breaks down the vision into manageable chunks. It celebrates the wins along the way even if there is much more to be done.

Currently, more than forty million people, many of them children, are trapped in slavery.[1] At what point should we celebrate? Do we wait until they're all free? No. We celebrate each victory.

Whatever your goal is, you can segment the task and celebrate the wins. If you're after personal development or a transformation of your marriage or a turnaround in your kids' behavior or a massive increase in your number of clients, how can you break down the end goal into bite-size wins?

Second, celebration lets you and your team know what the win *is*. This is really important. A team is built on that. For us the champagne bottle represented a win. Some visions are so big your team can get lost in the sheer size of them, overwhelmed by the responsibility and the size of the task, not to mention the anxieties that strike all of us about uncertainty in the economy, politics, and life.

Your team needs wins. Those wins build confidence. So they need to know what wins look like.

Third, celebration lets you know that change is possible.

A couple of years ago, we changed our celebration strategy. We met a girl who literally had been held in chains by her own mother, who had also sold her into prostitution and forced labor. What this girl experienced should not be allowed to happen. She was physically kept in chains, her freedom kept from her. We rescued her. She went through our Lighthouse program and the Dream Home, and now she is doing well. She is thriving. She no longer has a padlock.

We decided that every time someone was rescued and graduated our program, we would write the person's name on an opened padlock; then we affix those padlocks to the walls of our offices around the world. Those padlocks show me and our team once again that change is possible.

If you have decided to go after a huge goal, your vision may sometimes seem unattainable. Learning the art of celebration is one of the most important things you can do for your own life and for your team. We are often too hard on ourselves. We forget the wins because of the size of the work still left to do. But you and your team need to remember you're making progress.

To talk more about celebrating what you want to replicate, especially in the team setting, I would like to introduce Andrew Burton. Andrew has taught me a lot about work-life balance and how to handle success while maintaining family values. He has been a personal friend and mentor for many years, and he's also developed one of the best business models I've seen to date. Andrew is a master at encouraging his team and celebrating what he wants to replicate in his company. Here is his story.

Back in the 1980s I was a young man working in the corporate world in the UK. I was far down on the food chain, very frustrated with everybody else making decisions that I didn't necessarily think were good ones. I was discovering at the same time that I wasn't really cut out for the big corporate life as just a cog in the machine. I thought it would be great to be in control of my own destiny, rather than being subject to the whims of someone I didn't even know.

Soon after that discovery, an opportunity came along. My brother worked for an organization that was setting up a car rental business. They were looking to bring the master franchise of Thrifty Car Rental into England. I'd done some sales work, so my brother wanted to know whether I would be interested in heading up the sales at Thrifty.

Our beginning was inauspicious. I sold my wife's car to start up the business. We had the opportunity to buy the Thrifty franchise when I was only twenty-seven years old and didn't have much in savings. We had just bought a house, which we put on the line too, so the only asset we could sell was my wife's car. Plan B, if it all fell over in the first two years, was that we would go live with her mother. Happily my wife was 100 percent behind the plan, and it all worked out well.

CELEBRATE WHAT YOU WANT TO REPLICATE

What I'd most like to convey to you, dear reader, is the importance of developing your team. If I have an area of special passion in the commerce or ministry sector, I think it's how to grow and encourage your team—and how to spot things that could damage it.

It's important to surround yourself with people who are good at the things you're bad at. No shame there. No one is good at everything. That's just how it is. Being part of a team of people where your weaknesses are covered by their strengths is really what works.

That is exactly what I found in my brother. He was more entrepreneurial and braver, and I brought operational skills. Together we were very good complements for each other, which is why we stayed working together for so many years. We still work on business projects together after thirty years.

It's so important to find people with complementary skills. I wanted to run my own business, certainly, but not as "a complete man" on my own—rather, as part of a team.

Leadership That Builds the Team

I have seen two qualities that are effective for leaders of teams or companies. One is being a role model to your staff. Leading in such a way that they respect you means you model what you want them to be like and you don't constantly frustrate them.

Part of the reason I wanted to run my own business was that I got so frustrated by my bosses, but I just had to put up with it.

In large measure my leadership style is sort of a reaction to many of the ways my bosses operated that I didn't like.

You know this too. I'm guessing you've had good leaders and bad leaders. You have a fairly strong sense of what you'd like to emulate and what you'd like to never see again.

A principle in business, as in life, is that you must celebrate what you want to replicate. It's the same the other way round, really: what you replicate *is* what you celebrate. What you're seeing in your team is what you've encouraged. If your staff members are discouraged and bickering, you can look back and understand that somehow you—the leadership—have played a part in creating that behavior.

It's far better, I've found, to cultivate the attitude you want in the workplace through your actions and words as a leader than to try to undo a culture of negativity.

As a leader you will create an environment that is a reflection of what you bring to the party. You are a role model, for better or worse, so I recommend that you intentionally model the behaviors you think will best position your organization for success.

In the very early stages at Thrifty, we set out some strong values for the business. We said our core values were integrity, a strong work ethic, supporting one another, and working as a team. That's what we wanted to replicate.

Now, not everyone is going to like the values you model. When it comes to it, not everyone is especially going to like *you*. You may have to deal with people of this sort, and I'll speak to that later. But that's another benefit of modeling the values and attitudes you want to engender: it will expose those who are not aligned with you, and it's actually quite helpful to be able to identify those people.

The first pillar of leadership in my view is therefore to be a role model. The second pillar of good leadership is to understand that you are there to serve your staff.

For me this has always meant presenting to my team what it is we need to accomplish and then asking them what they need or what changes would enable them to do their jobs.

I think the key to serving your staff is to adopt the view that all your stakeholders, your team and your customers included, are actually your colleagues. If your staff sees you not as lording your authority over them but as being humble enough to seek to serve them, you will be an effective leader.

One of my mentors had this perfect ability to be firm in telling people what they couldn't do or what they were doing wrong but in such a gracious, gentlemanly way that even when you were being scolded, you left feeling good about it.

When adding new people to our team, I have held four priorities firmly in mind. All four are essential. If even one is missing, that person will not work out, I have found.

The first quality is integrity. If you can't trust your staff, you will find it difficult to manage or lead. Several of my interview questions are designed to get at the candidate's level of integrity. I try to find out whether it's one of their core values, because it certainly is one of mine.

The second quality is people skills. So many of the challenges in business happen because person A doesn't get along with person B. The question "Will this person fit in our team?" was more important to us than whether or not the person had terrific job skills. We were renting cars, after all, not building the

Large Hadron Collider, so we could train for many of the skills we needed our employees to have. The saying we used at Thrifty was "Hire the attitude; train for skills."

The third quality we looked for in a new hire was the capacity to demonstrate the ability to do the job, assuming we provided them with sufficient training. They didn't need all the skills for the job, as I've said. But they needed to look as if they would be able to do the tasks required of them.

The final quality I search for in a new hire is a strong work ethic. A lazy worker will be unpopular among the team members and will really hurt morale.

As far as possible, try to screen for these four qualities in your interview process.

When Things Get Difficult

I'd like to tell you that if your leadership style is stellar and all your new hires are top notch and you're modeling servanthood for your staff, everything will turn out great every day. But that's simply not so. In business, setbacks will come.

As a rule, entrepreneurs want to change the world. Often they see their way quite clearly to the change they want to effect. So when setbacks and failures come, they can become discouraged. Perhaps they thought God would be so excited that someone was finally acting on this vision that He would remove all obstacles and bring the dream into reality straightaway.

When big companies or production firms create a budget for a project, it's common practice to add a percentage because they know some things will not go to plan. It's actually included as a line item in the budget—that's how sure they are that things will go wrong.

We should take a lesson from these companies. Things will go wrong in your endeavor, whatever it is. And the bigger your dream, the bigger and more numerous your obstacles will be. If you plan on that now, if you make it a line item in your mental budget, it won't alarm you when it happens. You'll just get on with the business of bringing your vision to pass.

If you were to cut me open, my hope is that you would find the word *encouragement* somewhere on my innards. People thrive on encouragement, especially from their leaders.

I always tried to motivate my team with personal encouragement, meeting with key staff regularly one on one, reminding them of what they'd done well and offering to help them where they weren't doing well.

Public acclamation is another way to help your team. When somebody does well, share that across an email or at a team meeting or just in conversation. People thrive on knowing that they're doing well and that you appreciate their hard work. And it generates a lot of goodwill and loyalty.

Many times people move on to other jobs because they don't feel appreciated. You can help retain a team that works well together just by telling them regularly and authentically that you see their effort and like what they're doing. It doesn't take much to say, "I noticed you stayed late that night for three hours. How about you don't come in till ten tomorrow morning?"

Stronger Together

Where do solutions come from? I find that solutions come from people talking together around the table and sharing the challenge. There's an old adage that a problem shared is a problem halved.

At Thrifty we created teams in each area of the business. Each team consisted of four people from the head office and four franchisees. They would work together to find solutions to particular problems and to improve our operations and profitability. I think that decision, to create those teams, was one of the keys that made us so successful.

As you look around your organization, what problems are you currently facing and trying to solve on your own? If you decided you wanted to bring together a team to tackle the problems, how would you go about it? Who would you pull in?

I encourage you to give it a try. I know many entrepreneurs like to be the dashing hero riding in and solving everything in epic fashion. But you'll find there's less and less call for that sort of thing as you progress. Indeed, you may find that the person trying to be all things and fill all roles is actually the logjam. Consider whether you may need to get out of the way of your organization's success. There are those around you who can fantastically accomplish what you're only mediocre at—or truly terrible at. Let them bring their contribution to your vision.

Before we started having those meetings, we in the head office would often get frustrated when we rolled out a plan we thought was a great idea but then the franchisees rejected it or didn't use it. What these meetings showed me was that we weren't always seeing things clearly from our seats in headquarters.

I came to think of these meetings as the crucible for ideas. We'd put our "great" ideas in front of the four franchisees, and we'd start to hash them over together. The bad ideas would get chewed up and kicked out. I learned not to be frustrated by this but to see it as a rich reward. Look how much time and money they'd saved us all by identifying the flaws in our plan before we tried to roll it out across the organization! The good ideas were made even better by the same process. Just like a crucible for gold or silver.

I have to admit that I didn't like it when I would stand before a team and present an idea that they ended up not liking. It's often difficult to remove oneself from these things. How can their rejection of my brilliant idea not be on some level a rejection of me? And then I'd get defensive and hurt and would choose the wrong hills to die on.

I think that we all unfortunately have a sort of natural fear of what other people will think about us if we do or say certain things or come up with silly ideas. You have to be brave enough to present your new idea or your change and not feel deflated when somebody challenges it.

It's essential to be so comfortable with yourself that you're able to listen and not get defensive when someone challenges you. Not everyone's going to like your ideas—or, frankly, you—and that's OK. If they destroy your idea, well, that's brilliant, because it probably wasn't a good idea to begin with. It wasn't good enough to get through the crucible. That person who challenged you may have just saved your career or company.

I ran a football (soccer) team for many years with my sons, and for many of those years, we had a great team. But we had one poor lad who was not a terrific player. When he went on the pitch, we knew we were in trouble because he got railroaded no matter where we put him.

We usually put him as striker, because if he lost the ball at the other team's end, we still had midfield and defense to get it back. But we played him as left back in one game, and it was awful. We got hammered. That experience showed me that, in a team of eleven, if you have one poor performer—in this case, a lovely lad but a poor ballplayer—your team gets in trouble.

That proved to be my experience in business as well. If you have one poor performer, he or she can ruin the whole team. Because if you don't deal with that person, the good team members will eventually leave. You celebrate what you want to replicate, and if you tolerate bad behavior, *that's* the sort of behavior you're going to replicate.

I think there are broadly three categories of employees. There are some who are really good almost all the time. They're easy and fun to work with. Then you have another set of employees who are also easy. These are the ones who are just average. Not good or bad. But your company wouldn't miss them if they were gone. The difficult ones are the ones I call the "just enough employees." They do just enough to make sure they don't get sacked, but they don't do enough to keep the team happy. Dealing with those people before they disrupt your team is absolutely critical.

Think about your team. Do you have someone who is bringing you all down? You may like the person as an individual, or you may have great compassion for what that person has been through, but if you're honest, you know he or she is damaging your team. Is it worth losing your best team members over?

Have Faith

I have found my Christian faith extremely helpful in making sure I kept the correct balance of life and work. The life of an entrepreneur can become so consuming. So, both in terms of time and headspace, your life could become totally focused on that one thing, leading to stress and burnout.

My faith had a way of reminding me what was most important. It brought the proper perspective and taught me to not get too wrapped up in things that, in the end, didn't matter as much.

I also determined that I wasn't going to work on the weekends. I would work hard during the week, and that would be it. I would rather work later in the evenings, and if I had to, I could work again after the kids went to bed. Obviously there are times when you are very busy, and you have to work extra hours now and then. But for me my faith and being intentional about maintaining a life-work balance and Sabbath rest were vital principles.

My faith helped me in practical ways too. Before difficult or important meetings, I would pray for wisdom to make the best decisions. If I were bidding for a big rental contract, I would pray that I was getting the margins right and that I wasn't committing the franchise network to too onerous a contract.

My faith also offered me a plumb line in that it convinced me I needed to do the right thing each time. If there was some dispute going on with our franchisees, the *right* thing might be to return their money. Now, that wasn't the expedient thing from the profit/loss point of view, but it was the right thing to do.

How do you persevere when times get hard? Lean into your faith, protect and nurture your time with your family, and treat people the way you want to be treated. These are ways to celebrate what you wish to replicate.

I recommend you keep a healthy perspective by pursuing interests other than your enterprise.

My charitable work has been a very healthy outside interest for me. When you're involved in dealing with poverty in the third world and you hear stories of what other people are going through, your own concern begins to look more like a first-world problem.

It always helped me realize that the things I was fretting about really weren't worth it. That was definitely a useful perspective. It showed me that, yes, the issue was important but it wasn't the end of the world.

Climbing Out from the Lowest Moments

Soon after we went out on a limb financially with Thrifty, Black Wednesday hit. On Wednesday, September 16, 1992, the UK withdrew from the European Exchange Rate Mechanism. Investors withdrew, and money for investments vanished.

As it happened, my brother and I had just committed to buying four hundred vehicles from Ford. We were going to do so with investor funding. We were quite confident of the plan because we had three investors willing to fund the project. But then Black Wednesday happened. We had to buy these cars by a certain date or the deal was off. And if we couldn't get the cars to our network, we were sunk. That was definitely one of our lowest points.

My brother, Robert, and I sat in the office late one night. We had to buy the vehicles the next day. The first potential funder called and said, "Sorry. There's too much going on at the moment. We can't do it." The second company got back to us at about six thirty, only to pull out. We had one option left on the table. Robert and I looked at each other and said, "This could be curtains for us if we don't get a yes here." Fortunately that last supplier made an offer to fund the vehicles. It wasn't a cheap rate, though.

The second low point came after we'd been profitable for ten years, when there was a calamitous drop in the used-car market. At that point we owned over one thousand vehicles, and they fell in value overnight, wiping £1.2 million ($1.5 million) off our balance sheet and net worth, which put severe pressure on our relationships with our vehicle financing lenders.

Once again Robert and I found ourselves sitting in the office late at night. We came up with a first plan of action for what we would do if we couldn't make money, and then we came up with a second plan and a third. But we got through that one too.

That's when I found the value of talking to family, friends, and colleagues to come up with a plan to make difficult situations manageable so you can get through the low points.

What about you? Whom can you talk with when the stress is high and you want to walk away from it all? Cultivate those relationships. Be there for someone else who's going through it, and then perhaps it will soon be your turn to do the talking.

When it comes to it, there are times when even faith, talking with friends, and keeping a good work-life balance just aren't enough to keep you at it.

Perhaps it's not the most noble motive, but frankly the fear of letting people down kept me from quitting at my lowest point. Fear of letting down our franchisees, my brother, my wife. I have to say too that the prospect of losing my house was quite a good encouragement to stay at it. I didn't want to tell my wife, "Yeah, it's all over. I've lost the house."

You have a responsibility when you're employing people. Our franchisees had invested over £100,000 ($129,000) each into their businesses, and we'd made commitments to shareholders. It's that sense of duty that makes you think, *Well, this isn't great at the moment, but we need to keep going until we can find a way through.* Happily it got much better after that.

Learning from Mistakes

It's important not to beat yourself up too much when you make mistakes. You will absolutely make mistakes. Just plan for it. The unexpected truth is that we can always become better business leaders after we've made mistakes. If you take the time to learn from them and adjust, you'll be better off having made the mistakes than if you never had.

For example, we went to a new town where a franchisee wanted to open up a car rental business. We met with various people in the town, and one chap said to me, "Whatever you do, don't franchise with a gentleman named Bill Smith [not his real name]." He said, "He is no good. He's really a thug and a dangerous person." We thanked him and kept an eye out for Bill Smith, but we never came across him. We ended up franchising through a company owned by a man named John Jones (also not his real name).

About two months later, I got a phone call from somebody we'd talked to who said, "Why did you franchise with Bill Smith?"

I said, "We didn't. We franchised with John Jones."

"Ah," the person said, "I think you'll find that John Jones is Bill Smith in disguise."

Immediately after that, we began doing police background checks on all our franchise prospects. We got caught on that one, but I don't know how many times that experience has saved us from trouble.

On another occasion we went to court against a franchisee. It was such a hassle and such an expense. A complete mistake.

But from then on, my brother and I determined never to go legal when we had a dispute. We determined to keep meeting with the person until we found a resolution to the conflict. Once again a bad experience led to a practice that helped us greatly in our business going forward.

To Those Tempted to Quit

Sometimes I'm asked, whether in the business sector or in the missions or social justice arena, what I would say to someone who is on the verge of quitting.

I would say, "Don't rule out quitting."

Does that surprise you? You probably thought I'd say, "Come on; keep going; don't give up." And maybe that is what you need to hear. But the reality is that sometimes staying the course is not the correct choice.

A decision we had to make with our franchisees whose businesses were performing poorly was whether or not they should carry on. We had the option of funding them a bit if they'd run out of their own resources. But the other option was simply to let the franchises die. It was a different answer for different situations. Some franchisees found ways to carry on by themselves. Some carried on with our loans, which they staged repayments on. And to others we said, "No, it's time to quit."

To the person thinking of ending his or her run, I would say, "Make sure you've done everything you can to get through this. But if you have done it all and it's still not working, then maybe it's time to quit rather than put good money after bad."

One of my own maxims in business is that, preferably, you need to enjoy your work. That's the first thing. Making good money is the second thing. If both of those are in place, that's your utopian scenario, and you can go on for a long time.

Now, if you enjoy the work but you're not making money, it can still be worthwhile. You might just like the work for its own sake. If you are making money but you don't like what you're doing, that could be fine as well. If the financial payoff outweighs your lack of enjoyment, you can carry on for some time. But if you have the worst of both worlds, a double negative of not enjoying it and not earning enough money to make it all worthwhile, then I definitely think it's time to quit.

If you're not enjoying it and you're not making money, then all you have is the aggravation that comes with running a business. Who needs that? In that case, maybe there's something more fulfilling you can do to make money. Quitting may make you so much better off. Don't rule it out.

I have taken my own advice. After our successful run with Thrifty, I got into the health care sector, which is very different from the car rental business. I found out very quickly that I didn't actually like running a home care business on a daily basis—certainly not enough to do it for another ten years. So I exited that business. I quit. I could've pressed on, for sure, but I didn't want to. It didn't give me sufficient joy and remuneration, so I went on to other endeavors that would perhaps give me both.

Some people are frightened about walking away. Perhaps they feel that they have failed if they quit. But there's no shame in walking away if you're not enjoying it. There's something out there that is better for you, at which you can make more money or which is more enjoyable.

Now, dear reader, I have come to the end of my tale. I trust it has given you ideas for how to do business and, better yet, how to enjoy your life and do good in the world. Celebrate what you want to replicate, lean on your faith, keep proper perspective, and you should do well.

Your task is large, and your challenges can be daunting. Your team needs to know that progress is being made. Maybe break down the goal into smaller segments.

My attitude was better today. Well, that's a win.

My children are going to bed closer to when I want them to. That's a win.

My inbox is not quite as full as it was yesterday. That's a win.

Little by little you march toward your objective. Stop being so hard on yourself. Stop feeling the immense pressure of having to be perfect. We are works in progress.

There is a Bible verse that says we are to work out our salvation (see Phil. 2:12). Whether you have faith or not, none of us were born perfect. None of us are now perfect. We are just working things out.

It's good to celebrate the wins along the way. Celebrate what you want to replicate.

DISCUSSION QUESTIONS

1. What's a creative way you could celebrate with your team that both encourages them and reemphasizes your vision and goal?
2. What other organizations do you know that do celebration well, and what can you learn from them?
3. Do you both enjoy your work and find it financially satisfying? If one or both of those are missing, what could you do to improve the situation? Or is it time for a change?

IT'S OK NOT TO BE OK, BUT IT'S NOT OK TO STAY NOT OK, OK?

One of the greatest challenges about our culture at Hope for Justice is that we are very, very positive. Don't get me wrong: I love our positive culture. I have worked hard to generate the "Yes, we can!" spirit that imbues each person on our team. Being positive in a negative situation is not naive—it is leadership. We reject the negative, cynical, tearing-others-down culture we see around us. We are determined to build up others and be empowering.

But strange as it may sound, that type of positive culture can sometimes be a challenge. Why? Because it doesn't allow room for realism.

I lead an organization that grapples with some of the darkest acts humans can commit against other humans. We are up against people who are literally buying and selling children. Sometimes the children they're selling are their very own. Everywhere we work, we encounter the most broken, lost, and evil people in the world.

How can we as a team not have days when that simply gets to us? It's great to be happy and optimistic—you have to be that way, or you won't have hope that you can make a difference. But these are compassionate, loving people whose only hope is to bring release to the captive and liberty to the oppressed, so how can they go on being happy when so much oppression remains?

Sometimes, when the person who is feeling defeated meets with a person who is full of hope, the one who is low can be lifted up. But at other times the optimism can grate against the justified sadness the low person is feeling. And occasionally the person feeling low can feel a sort of peer pressure to put on a happy face.

We see so much despair and suffering that it would be wrong not to acknowledge it for what it is or not to acknowledge the fact that sometimes, as a team, we struggle. Dealing with people who are this broken can sometimes break us.

Here's a principle I've learned that will help you if you get to a similar place (it sounds a little funny, but it's entirely true): It's OK not to be OK, but it's not OK to stay not OK, OK?

My friend, it's OK to struggle. It's OK not to be perfect every time, not to be "fine." It's OK if you have struggled with anything—finances, relationships, jobs, family, weight, anxieties, mental health, or something else. Guess what? No one is OK all the time. And most of us, if we are being honest, would say we're not OK *much* of the time.

Many of us are facing a relentless attack on our well-being. The news bombards us with negativity. Social media invades our lives to the point of affecting relationships and our thinking. We are constantly faced with the sexualization of society and messages that we should be discontented with what we look like. Political, social, and gender issues are complex, and everybody seems furious about them. It all can begin to accumulate and feel as if it's too much to bear.

Then we read books from or about people who have achieved all that we have wanted to achieve, and we compare ourselves with them. We find ourselves wanting, and the despair mounts.

I shouldn't be thinking this, we say to ourselves. *I shouldn't be struggling. Lots of people have it worse than I do. I should be achieving so much more.* This perceived underachievement weighs us down to the point where we are exhausted from hearing our own thoughts. Exhausted from experiencing the challenges we face. And we just want to shut the curtains, close our eyes, turn up the music … and forget.

I just want to say to you right now, it's OK not to be OK.

I'm not endorsing pessimism, self-berating, or a victim mindset. I'm simply acknowledging that we all struggle.

It's OK not to be OK.

But it's not OK to *stay* not OK.

Pastor John Siebeling knows this. He's had very low times of his own, and he offers compassionate counseling to others who are having their own lows. Pastor John has learned to choose his opportunity carefully when talking to people who are—or will soon become—not OK:

I hate to see people, especially young pastors, hit a wall. I've been where they are. With the best of intentions, I used to try to warn them when I saw difficulties coming, to try to help them avoid some of the same challenges I faced. But I've also learned that some of the most powerful work God does can come in the difficult seasons of life and ministry. Some things simply can't be learned in the easy times—and some things we have to learn for ourselves.

That's the challenge. God's given these young pastors a dream, and they have their own expectations of how it will unfold. I don't ever want to be a downer for them. I want them to stay passionate—to have audacious faith and keep coming up with big plans. Sometimes they'll say to me, "Pastor John, we're believing God for this much growth over the next year or to launch this many campuses over the next five years."

Even if it seems unrealistic, I always try to encourage them and say, "Dream big, man! Absolutely believe God for that." You don't want to mess with their mojo—to be the realist who throws a wet blanket on their enthusiasm or sows seeds of doubt in their faith.

In my earlier days of ministry, when I was set on one of my latest and greatest ideas, even if someone had come up to me with a gentle spirit and all the wisdom in the world, I still probably would have pressed on full steam ahead, full of faith and believing we would be able to beat the odds. It's like when athletes have certain pre-game rituals they feel they need to do. You don't want to get in the middle of that. Just let them do their thing.

I encourage them, I believe the best for them … and then I check back in with those young pastors a few weeks or months later to see how they're doing. If they say, "Man, I didn't think this was how it was going to be," then I'm able to say, "Hey, that's totally normal. This is what everybody faces," and maybe I can give them a bit of wisdom then.

I was once cycling through a country in Europe as part of a fund-raising challenge. At one point, over a thousand miles in, we were cycling against the wind. Our backs were in pain, our legs were exhausted, our bottoms were … Anyway, you get the picture.

My friend Tom started to get a little agitated because his seat didn't fit him quite right and we didn't have time to fix it since we needed to finish at a particular time. He started complaining and even hitting the seat.

I began joining in, complaining about the pain and the wind and the length of the journey we still had to go.

He and I kept reeling off our frustrations, getting more and more annoyed with our situation and egging each other on. It didn't help us. If anything, it made the pain more painful and the wind even stronger. It sapped our energy and our determination. Yet we kept on with it. Our negativity was gaining momentum. It was building and building and building.

Until another of our friends cycling with us turned around and shouted, "Enough with your pity party!"

It was in that moment I realized it's OK not to be OK but it's not OK to stay not OK.

Human beings love a good pity party. We revel in it. When we have problems, we write our pity party invitations and share them with our friends on social media or over coffee or on text, and many people come join us. We get everyone together and talk about the things that are going wrong.

Yes, I understand. It feels good to vent frustrations, especially if there is someone who feels the same way. If you are not OK, that's OK.

But don't stay there.

Patrick Thompson of the band Rend Collective knows this very well.

I've known Patrick for many, many years. I remember being in a kitchen with Patrick years ago, before Rend Collective really got going. He'd been asked to be part of another band, and he turned it down. But soon after he did, that band had a hit song. And I basically told Patrick that he was a fool for turning down that band. This new Rend Collective thing he was thinking about wasn't really what he should be doing.

That was a really bad bit of advice I gave Patrick. Thankfully he never took me up on it!

I knew Rend before they were a band and have toured with them after they became a band. Rend Collective have been big supporters of Hope for Justice. Here's Patrick's story.

Rend Collective started in 2002 in Northern Ireland. We weren't a band at all then. We just worked with teenagers in the church. We noticed a trend among our friends who were in the eighteen-to-thirty-year-old bracket. They were graduating from school, going off to university, and facing challenges in their faith quite often.

We realized that part of it had to do with the fact that whenever you're in youth group, there's a lot of attention given to you. There's a lot of mentorship and guiding you through life. But when you graduate and leave the youth group, that support can disappear quite quickly. People were suddenly faced with real-life problems, like paying bills and trying to get a job. Some friends our age went through grief and hardship, and we even had friends who died.

A group of us were heartbroken over all this, and we wanted to do something to help young people after they got too old for the youth group but still needed support. We started a group that we called Rend.

The name was taken from a couple of Scriptures in the King James Version of the Bible. The first is from Isaiah: "Oh that thou wouldest rend the heavens, that thou wouldest come down, that the mountains might flow down at thy presence" (64:1 KJV).

And then the other Scripture is from Joel: "Rend your heart, and not your garments, and turn unto the LORD your God: for he is gracious and merciful, slow to anger, and of great kindness, and repenteth him of the evil" (2:13 KJV).

Basically Joel told us not to put on a religious show but to be open and vulnerable to other people. In this group we were against putting on anything fake. We were about coming together with that age group and being real and open and honest with one another. We were about doing life with one another. We wanted to walk together through these challenges as we all tried to figure out things like faith and life and work.

That group lasted probably five or six years. Near the end of that time, there was a core group of leaders who realized that we probably wanted to write some songs out of our experiences and for the type of person Rend had attracted. We were all musicians anyway.

Our members have changed a wee bit over the years, but now we consist of Gareth Gilkeson, Chris Llewellyn, Ali Gilkeson, Steve Mitchell, and me.

We started writing and singing to the group. There was no intention at all to be touring or anything of the like. We just thought, *Here's what we feel we should create*, and we threw it out into the world. It got picked up by some people, and then some more, and the journey continued from there.

Now we tour around the world and have eight albums with some songs that were quite popular. It's incredible, thinking about how far we've come.

IT'S OK NOT TO BE OK

Things were difficult for us from the start. Don't get me wrong: we were thrilled to be asked to play in different places. It hadn't been that long since I'd left school at eighteen with the intention of being a musician, but I had no idea what that was going to look like. I had no real plan either for how I was going to fulfill that dream. I probably would have been happy playing in wedding bands and pubs on the weekends, which is what I was doing at the time. So being asked around to perform was grand.

But those early years of touring were not easy. We tended to do the cheapest travel possible, of course. One time when we needed to get home from Sweden, it was an hour-and-a-half flight, but we couldn't afford to make it that far. We could afford to fly to London but no farther.

We ended up in Heathrow Airport trying to get all our team and equipment on three tubes (trains), which was a challenge in itself, and then taking three trains to Scotland and then the boat across to Northern Ireland. It took us thirty hours to get home instead of ninety minutes. Honestly I think it probably saved us only about £250 ($320) total, but we just couldn't afford to fly. After we got into Belfast at about five thirty in the morning, I got two hours of sleep and then went straight to work.

But it's that sort of shared hardship that bonded us, I think. I don't doubt that it has been the reason we have lasted this long. It's been over a decade since it all began, and we've seen a lot of other bands come and go in that time. The camaraderie of those tough times at the beginning has kept us together.

It's sort of been a pattern that God uses the hard times to bind us together. I think He also **chooses** the hard times to speak to us most clearly and to show us His heart. It's as if God is saying, "Hey, I know you're not OK right now, but that's OK. I'm with you when it's not OK, and I'm not going to let you stay not OK, OK?"

A good example of this is from 2010 when we were on our first tour of North America. We had borrowed a rubbish car to get to the airport in America. But on the way to the airport, at three or four in the morning, the car broke down. The battery died and we were stuck. We got a tow to the airport, but by that time we had to leave the car and run for the plane. We flew to Toronto to play some shows.

Two days later, we flew back to the States, and there was the car, still dead. We found somebody to come and replace the battery, and we put the old battery in the back of the car, where our suitcases were. That day we flew home to Northern Ireland. I opened my suitcase at home and found that battery acid had leaked through my entire suitcase, destroying every item of clothing I owned at that time. I remember opening the suitcase and pulling out white shirts that fell in half as I lifted them.

What was I going to wear to work? Much less to perform onstage?

At that moment I was not OK. I was pretty desperate, actually. But God made sure I didn't stay not OK. We had about three days at home before we were scheduled to head out again for a six-week tour. I had no clue what I was going to do. I had absolutely no clothes to my name. Then somebody at church walked up to me and gave me an envelope with £200 ($250) in cash and said, "I just felt like God told me you needed this."

Wrestling with Being Not OK

It has to be OK not to be OK. You have to wrestle.

When I was very young and in school, I was part of a band that was not successful in any way whatsoever. But I felt that God was calling me out of that group because He had different goals for me. I believed God wanted me to do music, but I also believed that the current band was not going to take me where He wanted me to go.

I left that band, probably at age sixteen. And then, annoyingly quickly—suspiciously quickly after I left—that band became quite successful. They're still out there now, touring all over the world. They have sold I don't know how many records, and they're very, very popular.

I watched this happen as I was sitting in Northern Ireland without a band and without any prospects. I was confused, as you can imagine. I believed God had called me to be a musician, and I remember thinking, *I made a mistake. I'm in the wrong position. I have totally misunderstood God.* I went into a season where I felt silence from God. I was not OK.

During that time I talked to my friend Lindsey about it all. When she heard of my sadness and frustration, she would say, "Oh, but it's OK to be in the wilderness. You know that, right? It's OK to be in the wilderness."

I honestly did not understand what she was saying. She would say it and sort of laugh, and that would be the end of the conversation. This happened three or four times. She just kept saying, "But remember, it's good to be in the wilderness." I thought she was talking complete nonsense.

This season went on for a year. I felt incredibly down about my decision. When I talked to somebody else about what Lindsey had told me and how annoying I thought she was, this person said, "Well, do you not understand what she's talking about? If you're in the wilderness, it's like when Jesus was walking in the wilderness. It's an opportunity for you to rely on God. Hearing from God is quite difficult sometimes. The wilderness helps filter out the noise. Lindsey was saying that it's OK to have nothing. It's OK to be in the wilderness, because you're in a situation where you have no choice but to rely on God."

I heard a preacher talk about how the *testing* of our faith produces endurance, from the first chapter of James. We're to consider it great joy when our faith is tested (see vv. 2-4). At that point in my life, James's words sounded like complete nonsense to me too.

The preacher said that a silversmith heats the raw silver until it melts, because then all the impurities float to the top. The silversmith skims away those impurities. This is called "testing" (and I believe this is what James had in mind). Again and again the silversmith does this until all the impurities are gone. How does he know when they're all gone? At some point at the end of the process, he can see his own reflection in the silver. And that's how he knows the process is done and the silver is pure.

To me that's a beautiful picture of going through the times when you're not OK. That process is an opportunity for problems and mess and dirt within us to rise to the surface so we can deal with them and our impurities can be skimmed off. That's why it's OK not to be OK. Because when you are OK, the things that need to be dealt with remain below the surface and invisible. But when you go through the furnace, they rise and God skims away those things.

Until, in the end, God can look at us and we will reflect Him brilliantly because of that season when we were not OK.

God Loves to Talk When We're Really Listening

Probably the lowest moment I had in Rend Collective came fairly early in our American touring. We had basically committed to ourselves that we would do whatever it took to get some sort of foothold in the American market. Because we felt that if God was calling us to do this full time, the only way that would be financially viable would be to work in America for at least part of the year, since it's such a big market.

Also, getting traction in the States is a great way to get your music out there. If you can have some influence in America, it really assists with getting the music into the rest of the world. We felt that if God wanted the songs to travel farther, then America seemed like the logical place to start. We worked hard at that for a number of years.

In the 2010–12 time frame, we couldn't afford to fly back home to Northern Ireland very often. In January 2012 we were in Atlanta, Georgia, and I remember it became apparent that we weren't going to be able to get back home for an awfully long time. We were committed to so many concerts I had no idea when I would get back again. I suppose I'm sort of a ridiculous bird, because I struggled with being away from home for more than about two weeks.

I slipped into a season of a bit of depression. At that time we were living in our manager's basement in Atlanta. Four of us were sleeping on air beds in one room in his basement. I remember not wanting to leave that room. I couldn't face going outside and trying to build relationships or trying to make any sort of ties to the States. I was longing to be home so much that I felt I was betraying Northern Ireland if I made any friendships in the States.

Hiding down in the basement, longing for home, afraid I was betraying my homeland ... that was definitely my lowest moment.

I look back on it now, and I think it was OK that I wasn't OK. Most people could understand why I might've felt that way, I think. It was a hard time, and it's natural for a soul to feel low. But God doesn't want us to settle in that place, and I knew it wasn't healthy for me. It's OK not to be OK, but it's not OK to stay not OK.

At that point the other guys in the band were emotionally healthier than I was. They were making friends and investing time in a church for that season. Basically they were trying to make the best of a difficult situation. I felt isolated and thought nobody understood how I felt. I probably seemed like a struggling teenager even though I was actually in my midtwenties. All I wanted to do was watch *The Office* (American version) on Netflix as many times as possible.

Chris eventually called me out and said, "I can tell you are probably feeling depressed. And I understand what that's like." It was quite encouraging to know that somebody was hearing my very quiet cries for help.

On the few occasions we managed to get back home, we had several encounters with people in Northern Ireland who shared prophetic messages with us. One man said, "God wants to say He's really pleased with what you're doing. And He understands your pain. He can see the difficulty you're going through. He's aware, Patrick. But He's very pleased. He's very happy with what you're doing."

God loves to talk to us when we're really listening, doesn't He? It's OK when we're not OK, but He's not OK with leaving us that way.

Those things lifted me out of that depression. It also helped that Gareth and Ali, who were married to each other and in the band together, were able to rent a house in Atlanta. When they left, having more room for the rest of us down in the basement really helped, even though Chris and I ended up living in that basement for another year.

I made more healthy choices after that. I got involved in the church, and we ended up leading a college youth group that was a bit like Rend for a short time. It was hard to be consistent because of our travel schedules, but we invested in that as a team, which was good. The more relationships I had with people in the church, the more helpful it was.

RELENTLESS PURSUIT

Our home church realized it was a difficult season for us. On more than one occasion, the church in Northern Ireland raised a bit of money to get me home. That was very helpful.

After that season, while I was somewhat involved creatively in writing music for the band, I started to spend most of my time managing the touring schedule and working with the crew we traveled with. I also looked after the financial side of things, planned marketing campaigns for tours, and did some social media marketing. Learning new skills broadened my horizons, and that's always good. To avoid being not OK, I had to find a way to contribute again. That was definitely a big change.

But honestly I have gone through times of depression over the last ten years. Many times. There are times during the year when I struggle to the extent that it affects my work. And then there are times when I find I'm contributing and excited to steer the ship in a particular way. It's an ongoing up and down. But none of the downs have been as low as that moment in the basement.

When Things Get Difficult

One way to overcome hardship is not to have it in the first place. There are things you can do to protect yourself from troubles that might otherwise come.

Our origins were in that Rend group in Northern Ireland. We were about walking authentically together with God. And we definitely wanted to bring that sort of ethos to the band. We deliberately cultivated it.

Four of us have been in the band from the word *go*, so we don't have to cultivate that ethos deliberately among ourselves anymore. We've been through thick and thin together, and we are essentially family. We certainly spend a lot more time with one another than we do with our actual families.

We also have a larger team of people involved in what we do. We can't do this on our own. We have crew members, team managers, booking agencies, and various other people we work with on a regular basis.

We're intent on the whole team being inclusive. Everyone is welcome, and we're always looking for ways to expand our team and the community. But we're quite protective of our community as well.

Because we are a traveling community and the smallest piece of negativity in what we do can quickly run through the entire group, not everyone is a good fit to travel with us, even though everyone is welcome in our community. When you're on the road together, when you're tired or run down, the tiniest thing can push people over the edge.

We all love our community, and we're scared it could be damaged by somebody. We're a bunch of fragile people. When you travel as much as we do, you're really only as happy as your relationships are.

That's why, when we have relational problems inside the community, they are swiftly dealt with. If anybody is thinking a little too much of him- or herself, or if anybody is saying negative things, it's quickly stepped upon, because we have to be protective of the group. I think everybody on the team has at some point been called up on the way he or she is acting. I know I have.

You might think we have a long list of rules for traveling with Rend Collective. But really, we have only one: don't be an idiot.

I don't mean that in terms of being a stupid person. I mean, don't be unpleasant. I'd like to put this in big stars so everyone would see it, but I don't think my management would sign off on that.

But that's the one key rule: don't be annoying. We're all in this together. We're all away from home; we're all uncomfortable; we're all not having the easiest life in the world. So just realize everyone's in that situation. If you're uncomfortable or you're having a hard time, just know that everybody else is in the same boat as you. We're in this together, and we're only as strong as we are together.

Outside of that, we just try to model the behavior we want everyone to adopt, and we hope that is picked up.

Another way we avoid hard times is to build in a certain amount of rest and downtime. That's one thing when you work your sort of eight-to-five office job, but it's another matter when you travel for a living.

For us it all comes down to rest. But that is something that we are pretty terrible at getting, right? So we've learned to make and hold one rule: we take Decembers off.

That is crucial for what we do. Because we're in a position now where there are lots of families involved. Back when we started, over twelve years ago, it was basically just the four of us against the world. It was just us, so could travel anywhere for any amount of time. We had no ties. But now there are wives and kids involved.

And especially during the holidays, we all have different things that we to do. Chris and Steve have both married American girls. So they need to spend time with their Northern Irish families and their American families. It's just so important that we protect our Decembers. Honestly, come October or November, we're almost at our wits' end anyway. I couldn't imagine not having those weeks off. December is a time when we just don't do anything. I especially try to work as little as possible.

Taking Decembers off is how we stay OK and regain the ability to climb out of it if we're not OK.

We have a few other rules related to rest. We've learned that we can't do more than five shows a week. It turns out that doing six or seven a week is a terrible idea.

Whenever we're in America, Nashville is our home base. That's because Chris's wife lives there. So we try to make sure that every Monday, Tuesday, and Wednesday, we get back to Nashville, if at all possible. And if we can't all get back there, we'll make sure that Chris has a flight back.

Then, as soon as a tour is finished, it's just understood that the day it ends, my wife, Jude, and I are going to fly straight to Northern Ireland, because we need that, so we protect a few weeks off. The goal is to come back feeling refreshed and to have a refreshed vision as well.

When we're on tour, Jude and I quite often just need to get away from the venue during the day and spend some time just the two of us. Most tours have us playing in city arenas every day. Usually, within a five-minute walk of our hotel, we can find somewhere to get a cup of coffee. We just try to find a wee bit of time for us where we can go and connect as people and not be in work mode.

We also strive to keep in touch with our home church in Northern Ireland. We listen to the podcasts, which is quite lovely to be able to do.

To Those Tempted to Quit

I've been given what I believe is sound advice, which is that God doesn't just close a door. More often than not, you find that He's actually opening another door.

There have been times I've thought, *I'm not sure how much longer I can do this. This is very difficult. This is not easy.* Then I remember that advice, and I realize that just because something is hard doesn't necessarily mean that the door is closed. I think you'll probably know whenever it's time to move on. I think you'll know when God has completed His vision for you in this place or in this season and He's calling you to something else.

With some regularity I'll just check in with God. I'll ask Him whether we're still doing the right thing and we're still in the center of God's calling. I check in to ensure that He's not calling us to something new.

And if I do think He might be done with me here and moving me on to the next thing, I don't decide that quickly. I go through a period of testing and waiting and listening. Sure, someone might be offering something that is intriguing. But that doesn't mean there's definitely an open door there that God has opened. So I think it's vital to give God an opportunity to speak into that ... and to really listen.

If there's something on your heart that you feel He's calling you to, ask Him directly about it and wait for an answer. If you don't get a clear answer but you still feel it on your heart, look for a way to take a step in that direction. Take that step and then stop again and say, "God, am I going in the right direction?" And give Him an opportunity to respond. If you don't have a clear answer yet but you still feel it in your heart, then take another step. And then check with God again.

If you're walking like that, always wanting God's will, I don't think God will let you walk too far in the wrong direction. If you're inviting Him to speak to you, I don't think He'll let your foot wander too far from the path.

I've heard people speak about quitters, campers, and climbers. Quitters say, "I'm done! I don't want to be in this job or this church or this marriage anymore!" There are also always climbers. These are the people who want to go farther and faster. Climbers say, "I want to achieve more, and I never want to stop achieving!"

But the third kind of person is whom you're in danger of becoming when you are not OK. It's OK not to be OK, but you need to be careful that you don't start camping out in that land of not-OK-ness. If you live in a not-OK mind-set, you may never move on from there. You will find yourself camping with other campers, who only amplify your miseries, and you may never escape.

Kevin Kim knows about how the campers can accumulate and surround you and how they can tempt you to become a quitter.

> We had a full-on coup d'état in the youth department where I was working. The parents of the opposition group had their teens all sit in the front rows on Sunday mornings in the youth service. The first time it happened, I thought, *Oh, this is a pleasant surprise. They're all here early and ready to go.* But then when I got up to preach, with the timing and precision of the Russian Olympic synchronized swimming team, in unison they all took out their headphones, put them on, turned on their music, took out books from their book bags, and proceeded to do their homework in front of me for the duration of the service. This went on for months. Good times.
>
> This was a huge cause of tension in my marriage. My wife and I argued about this almost every night for the entire first year of our marriage. Every night my wife would tell me this was

not worth it, we were wasting our time and our energy here, and we should leave. And every night I would tell her that we don't quit just because things are hard. Move on if they fire you. Move on if God calls you out. But you never move on just because it's hard.

Here are a few things I have learned about how to progress from not being OK.

First, find the right people to surround yourself with when you're not OK. You are a by-product of your environment. Choose your environment well. Don't send out pity party invitations. Send out invitations to those who can help you climb out of your heavy emotions. Whom do you go to when you are feeling low? Do you go to climbers, who will offer you encouragement? Do you turn to quitters, who will only tell you to give up? Or do you look for campers, who will reinforce your mind-set that says, *Don't deal with it?*

Those around you have the ability to pull you up, tear you down, or stop you from moving forward. A friend never tears you down. A friend only pulls you up—even if doing so might sometimes feel unkind. A hard truth spoken by a loving friend is far preferable to kind words from someone who wants you to remain defeated. So choose your environment well.

Second, if you lose your ability to laugh, you lose your ability to act. There is something about joy that is intrinsically linked to strength, hope, and creativity. If you want to be more than OK, if you want to sustain your momentum and pursue your impossible, you have to learn to laugh. I know this sounds silly. But I can think of hundreds of examples from Hope for Justice when laughter has done my soul good. It has helped sustain the momentum to keep building.

Third, guard your thoughts. There is a proverb that says, "As [a man] thinks within himself, so he is" (Prov. 23:7 NASB). What are your thought patterns right now? What does your self-talk sound like? When you are not OK, do you rehearse your negative thoughts as Tom and I did on our bicycles? Do you have a pity party with yourself? *They never loved me. They never really believed in me. They never wanted me to succeed. They never …*

In your self-talk, practice rehearsing truths rather than lies. Find some positive anchor thoughts you can always go back to when you face stress or hardship. Write down these well-constructed truths that build confidence, health, and positivity, and then refer to them when you're not OK.

I know this sounds simple. I'm a simple guy. Your thoughts affect your attitude, and your attitude determines the course of your life.

It is OK not to be OK, but in order for you to be more than OK, make sure you surround yourself with good people, make sure you laugh and deliberately look for joy, and make sure you remember that your positive thoughts are the most powerful weapon you have to sustain you so you are more than OK.

DISCUSSION QUESTIONS

1. Describe a time when you were not OK. How long did that time last, and what helped you finally emerge from it? Or have you emerged?

2. Patrick's friend told him that it was OK to be in the wilderness. What does that mean to you, and have you found it to be true?

3. What's a strategy you need to have in place to ensure you don't stay not-OK but move on toward your goals?

REMEMBER THE WHY BEHIND THE WHAT

By now you will have gone through how you are going to shape your words, you've asked questions of your frustration, you've innovated and come up with new concepts, you are owning your zone, you're attracting a tribe with your vibe, you are celebrating the wins, and you've realized that it's not going to be OK all the time.

There will be challenges along the way to your goal. Why? Because greatness costs.

You want to do something extraordinary with your life? It's going to cost you. You want a great marriage, a great family? You want to change the world? It's going to cost you.

And when you get to the point when you think, *I simply cannot do it anymore*, and you are ready to pack everything in, remember that greatness costs. You've heard some of my failures, and you've heard from several of my friends who have contributed, all of whom would attest that they have failed many times too.

As we strive toward our goal, we stumble and fall. The "what" of how we try to reach our "why" is not flawless. But that isn't really the point.

Let me tell you: the what that you do is going to drain you. It is going to take everything from you. Because what is a taker. What wants to rob you of your energy and vision.

But let me introduce you to a friend of mine who will help you through the driest of seasons and the biggest of challenges. This friend is a little person I call why.

The why behind the what is what gives you energy. Your why is what gives you purpose. Your why is what gives you passion. The why you are pursuing is one of the most important discoveries you can make.

Your why is attractive to your tribe, absolutely. But it's more than that. Your why is what helps *you*, like a close friend, through your darkest days.

Someone else who understands the power of a big why is Kevin Kim:

> I think one of the most important things you can do as a leader is to discover, articulate, codify, and communicate your why. Go to sleep to it at night and wake up to it in the morning. Put it on repeat for your team.
>
> Simon Sinek gave a TED Talk called "How Great Leaders Inspire Action."[1] His main premise

is that the differentiator between leaders and causes that fail versus ones that succeed is *why*. Great leaders have a clear concept of why to inspire people with, to bring the best work out of their teams, and to keep them going through failure and tough times.

I have the privilege of working with a great visionary leader in Francis Chan. When I first met Francis several years ago, I was working at a fantastic job and living in a nice neighborhood with great schools for my kids.

And then I had lunch with Francis.

At this lunch he said to me, "Why don't you leave your great job and great neighborhood and come help me plant churches and ministries in the most violent area of San Francisco? It's a dangerous neighborhood. The schools are bad. But that's where the Church needs to be."

So we did. And the moral of the story is: never have lunch with Francis Chan.

Actually these have been some of the most powerful and fulfilling times of my life. And the why Francis gave me to move, the vision he cast, was to reimagine Church—to bridge the gap between what the Church is now and what the Church could be according to Scripture.

You see, that's a why to sacrifice for, to get you excited in the morning, to keep you working through the frustrations and the failures. Over the past six-plus years in planting We Are Church, we've had many, many ups and downs. We've faced incredible headaches and heartaches doing ministry in San Francisco. We've had people turn back to a life of drugs and addiction after years of discipleship. We've had leaders walk away and criticize us. And we've had long periods of seeming fruitlessness for all our prayers and efforts.

If our team of pastors didn't have a strong and established sense of why, we would have all quit at some point in the last six years of church planting.

If you don't constantly put vision on repeat for yourself and for your team, if you don't connect the dots in a regular, systematic, and intentional way, you're going to drift, you're going to lose motivation, and eventually you're going to tap out.

Now I have the honor of introducing two friends of mine who are highly successful entrepreneurs and who also happen to be sisters: April Pointer and Jen Jordan.

April Pointer is a leader of incredible integrity. She's well thought, and to meet her, you would not believe how successful she is. She's built an outstanding business from the ground up, but you would not know it when you meet her. She's just real and sincere and not overly impressed with herself.

Jen Jordan is an incredible friend to me, a great supporter of Hope for Justice, and someone who has developed a really successful business. She has an amazing heart for people. One of the things I really appreciate about Jen is that not only is she incredibly successful; boy, does she make me laugh.

April's and Jen's thoughts are presented together here, and their wisdom is highly instructive. First they relate how they got into the health-supporting industry they've done so well in.

Back in 2009 my (April's) husband really needed some immune support. We were frustrated with the health care system in general and were looking for more natural remedies than pharmaceuticals. We encountered Young Living through its natural essential oils. We tried them, and they worked marvelously. We became avid product users for two years.

During that time a friend whom I'd gotten interested in the oils asked me to come talk to her other friends about them. She felt I was a good teacher and had experience with the oils, and she wanted to give that to her circle. I was reluctant but finally agreed, and we put together an evening in which I would talk about the product and offer the oils for sale or order.

Well, the event went far better than I'd expected. I made a significant amount of money that night just by talking to people about what was working for my family to stay healthy. I was completely blown away. I thought, *Wow, these people so desperately want natural health in their houses. And I can actually get paid to talk about this? What is this? This is crazy!*

That's when I saw a way for us to begin working to improve our financial situation. We were really, really in debt. We had been smart with our money. We'd used advice from Dave Ramsey and Crown Financial, and we didn't foolishly spend. But we were just drowning in debt.

And then, with that one evening event, I sort of woke up. I thought, *Wow, we could actually get out of debt with this. If I could earn an extra $500 a month that we could put toward retiring our debt, that would be huge.* Our lives were not really working at the time. We were a one-income family, a homeschool family. My husband was gone twelve to fourteen hours a day and saw the kids maybe two hours a day.

Our start wasn't some huge desire to change the world. We just needed to get help for ourselves, and this seemed like a way to try to get it.

Now, something like ten years after that moment, our situation is completely different. I have people above me in what we call our "upline," and I have many people below me in my "downline," and a portion of the earnings from my downline comes to me. I am humbled to have one of the biggest downlines in Young Living right now.

I started teaching classes with that friend. And it just led from one thing to another, all based on a friend telling another friend and having people over in our home.

Along the way I got my sister interested in essential oils. I'll let her take up the story now.

I (Jen) am so grateful April introduced me to the world of essential oils.

My involvement with Young Living began in a similar way to April's. When you find something you're passionate about, you tend to share your story with the people you care about. I just started talking about what changed my life, and people started asking, "How can I get that in my life too?" April introduced me to the product about ten years ago. But I wasn't convinced right away. I actually laughed at her and told her she was crazy. I think I even told her that the health aspects of it weren't real.

And then I got pregnant with my third child. This was our surprise baby. By this point I had started caring more about what I was putting into my body. So I decided to give natural wellness a try. When I started using the product, I realized that this is real. This really works.

Kind of inadvertently I started talking to people about it. My approach was just that I knew the product could help people. People jumped on that, and with April's help I got into the business, and she was very intentional about helping me grow a business. Now I too have one of the larger downlines in our organization, and things are going very well.

REMEMBER THE WHY BEHIND THE WHAT

The business I (April) am in is all about helping people. It's wonderful to work in an industry when your why is to directly benefit the well-being of others.

From a very young age, I'd been interested in the medical field. As an undergrad my goal was to become a veterinarian. But I can remember the moment when that all changed.

In college I was in a medical club for pre-med and pre-vet students. One time we had the amazing opportunity to go down to a hospital and watch open-heart surgeries. I remember walking into that front lobby and being struck by something I saw: right there in the cardiac hospital was a restaurant from a very famous fast food franchise.

That was my light bulb moment. In the heart hospital was a place that sold heart attacks in a box. I remember thinking, *The medical industry … some of them are not on our side. Some of them are not actually on the side of health, not if they're allowing this food to be served right here.* All I could think was that this restaurant was job security for these cardiologists.

I didn't know what to do with that revelation. But I knew then and there I didn't want to be part of that thinking. I actually changed my degree plan from veterinary medicine to nutrition.

My why was that I wanted to be someone who really was on the side of the patients and their health. To be honest, though, my other why at the outset was to get out of the debt we were in. As I mentioned, medical bills were mounting and we were drowning. When I found early success in helping people in improving their health and improve our financial situation, it was a wonderful marriage of two whys.

Then, after about the first four years of building my business, as success came and we paid off our debt, I started finding that my motivation was shifting. Now that the heavy load of debt was off our backs, we found that we wanted to be able to give more, both to our kids and to others around us.

For example, we'd always wanted to give a car to a single mom. It's a strangely specific intention, I know, but we'd always wanted to do it. Finally we were able to do that. Later, we heard about another single mom whose church had just bought a house for her family. But they asked for help in furnishing it, so we were able to get them a washer, a dryer, and a fridge. We also give our support to Hope for Justice. Giving is our why now.

It's similar with my sister too.

It was because of April's ongoing medical needs that, as a child, I (Jen) wanted to become a doctor. We were in and out of hospitals my whole childhood, and I wanted to be part of that medical world that was helping my sister.

I entered college and began my journey toward a biochemistry degree, with medical school as the next thing in the plan. But about two and a half years into it, I realized that the life of a doctor was not what I wanted. I didn't want to live on call. I didn't want to finance half a million dollars for medical school. I wanted to have kids someday. And I wanted to be home with my kids, but I didn't think that could be compatible with being a doctor.

So I sort of handed that dream to God. I got a degree in something else, got married, had babies, and stayed home with them. I was super fulfilled in that role as a mom. But it's so amazing that now, after I was introduced to these products that help people's health so much, I've sort of gotten my original dream back too. I'm not a doctor, of course, but with natural products I'm able to support the wellness of people around me.

The why I had as a child is the why I have now. It doesn't look like what I thought it would look like. I don't practice medicine. I don't prescribe. But I'm able to equip people with information that's changing their health for the better.

It's so important to tap into your why. Why are you doing this? Whatever your job or organization or project is, you have to have a motivation you believe in. Why I'm doing what I'm doing may be completely different from why you're doing what you're doing, but when things get harder, it's so important to remind ourselves of why we started.

Sometimes your why changes. That's what April was saying about starting out somewhat because of financial reasons but doing it now to help others. The why I had when I started is different from the why I have today. The needs I had when I started are met now. Those are gone.

Sometimes I think, *Hey, we don't need more money. Things will keep going on nicely even if I step back. So why don't I quit?*

But my why pulls me back every time.

I'm involved with many causes and initiatives now, including helping fund people's adoption efforts. Also, part of our desire to serve the orphans and the widows, to connect kids with those who will love and protect them, is fulfilled in the work we do with Hope for Justice against human trafficking.

Whenever I start thinking about quitting, my mind goes right to the thought of how many adoptions we could enable and how many girls in Cambodia we could free if I made even more money. When I know that there are orphans everywhere and girls and boys in slavery all over the world and that I could place them in a home or rescue them just by writing a check, how could I ever think about quitting? My why keeps me going and gives me so much joy.

And honestly my why goes beyond the girls and boys who are being rescued now. It's also about their future kids and their future grandkids. It's about a generational impact I can have in the world. That's my why, and it's a big one.

Both Jen and I (April) have gotten to very good places with our businesses. But it hasn't all been picnics and parades. For me, while many of the challenges have been external, some of the toughest setbacks and obstacles have been internal.

I used to have very negative self-talk. I used to spend a lot of time wanting things I didn't have. If somebody talked about going on vacation somewhere, I would think, *I would really love that too.* But I would shut down the thought immediately. I'd hear myself thinking, *Yeah, but that'll never happen for me.*

One day I finally realized what I was doing to myself with my words. I decided to start developing the habit of being thankful for what I do have. This helped me move away from constantly wanting what I didn't have, and it positioned me so that I set my mind on the good things I did have.

With gratitude came generosity. As we grew in gratitude, my family naturally wanted to give more. I realized that we didn't have to wait until I was wealthy to give generously of what we had. Generosity greatly improved my mental health and my over-all emotional well-being.

The secret to gratitude and generosity is moving away from a mind-set of lack and toward a mind-set of abundance. If you think there's not enough money or success or whatever else to go around, you'll constantly be hoarding and stingy. You won't be able to give, because what if you give to others and there is no more to come? That's what a lack mind-set will do to you.

But if you consider yourself always in a state of abundance, then you're positive there is plenty all around you that will flow back to you. That's when you can let things go easily and you can give them away generously.

For me (Jen) the biggest obstacle early on was the thought that people were not always going to be pleased with me. I knew I would daily disappoint people. I really didn't want people to be upset with me. That people-pleasing would have held me back and put me out of the game or kept me small. But I had a big why, so I worked on these internal roadblocks. It's so strange that our own issues can be the things that block our greatness.

Another thing I had to do to keep moving forward when things got tough was to learn to adapt and innovate. You can't live by staring into the rearview mirror.

April, we all had to innovate a few years ago, didn't we?

Up until 2014 I (April)—and all of us in the essential oils industry—had been able to talk about how these products were very effective in treating medical conditions and diseases. We'd been responsible about sticking to claims that could be substantiated, but others in our industry were not. Some other companies were making all kinds of outlandish and unsubstantiated claims about their products, and consumers were getting hurt.

As a result, new government regulations were added to the industry. It became illegal to make healing claims regarding the effectiveness of essential oils. From then on, a product had to be officially approved as a classified drug before anyone could call it a cure or a treatment that could mitigate disease.

When that change happened, we all took a huge hit. People stopped talking about essential oils in general and Young Living in particular. None of us in the organization knew how to promote our products anymore. Their usefulness hadn't changed, but how we talked about them had to.

That was definitely the low point for me. And not just me. Everybody in Young Living was kind of stuck. How could we still promote and sell our product but not talk about disease?

We had to reinvent ourselves. We had to innovate or die.

It took a while, but we learned to start talking about how oils help regulate emotions. We started talking about how to cook with the oils. We gave DIY talks about how to make these fun little roller bottles with your own blend of oils, and they became all the rage for a while. Instead of talking about healing and cures, we found we could talk about how essential oils support health and wellness.

This setback actually became a good thing for us. Before the new regulations, three people had shown up at my house at different times with a medical emergency instead of going to the emergency room. I'd been so outspoken about my successful experiences with the product. I remember telling those people, "Get in the car and go to the ER ... but here is a list of oils to use as you drive."

I chose to see this huge setback as an advantage. Thanks to these new regulations, I didn't have to be responsible for anyone's health. I didn't want people's health on my conscience anyway, and now I wasn't even allowed to make suggestions. I told my whole team, "This is a great thing. Let people be their own advocates for their health. It empowers them. They look things up themselves instead of contacting us!"

As with Jen, my own chief obstacles were ones I carried around inside me. For example, I used to ignore my emotions and disappointments and pretend they didn't exist. I would bottle them up and whistle a happy tune and just keep going. But that usually ended up going badly, because I'd blow up at some point, often on someone I really wasn't upset with.

I knew that had to change. I didn't want to be my own biggest obstacle. I had to work through it, but I finally came up with a system that works for me. Now, when I'm frustrated, I don't ignore my frustration. Instead of trying to mask it or cover it up, I let myself wallow in it for a time.

I know that sounds really bad. But I've found it's vital to let myself feel the feelings that go along with what's happened. I have to feel them before I can move on from them. It's sort of like catch and release in fishing.

When something goes wrong or someone says something unkind about me, I would normally have stuffed it down, gotten busy with something else, harbored resentment, and then exploded somewhere down the line. But now I let myself really feel it. I'm honest with how much it hurt. I look at it for what it is and I acknowledge how it feels. I let it sting.

But—and this is important—I set a time limit on the disappointment. After I've had a few hours or a day to feel sad about it and acknowledge my feelings, I focus not on what happened but on what can *be*, now and in the future.

In the same way, I've found that so much of my ability to relentlessly pursue my vision comes from managing my self-talk. When things go wrong or when someone is unkind, when you face all kinds of disappointments and setbacks, they can create so much self-doubt. You have to learn to manage your internal thoughts if you want to stay focused on the future.

You absolutely must stop your negative self-talk. Most people don't even realize they're talking negatively to themselves. That inner critic has been with them so long they don't even realize it's there anymore. But that kind of internal monologue is toxic.

The first thing you have to do is even notice that you're doing it. You have to catch yourself being a critic of yourself (and others) before you can ever hope to gain control over it. Pay attention to your thoughts. Notice the messages you're giving yourself even as they race across your mind. Write them down and stare at them. You'll start hearing the messages: *I'm lazy* or *I'm a bad mom* or *I'm broken* or *I have no self-control.*

I think you'll be shocked at what you catch yourself saying inside. Then again, you won't be shocked at all, because you'll recognize that you've been saying these things to yourself for years.

The next step, once you've noticed that you have this inner critic, is to separate yourself from it. It's not you that's saying these things. Not really. It's a voice inside you that you've picked up from other people or wrong interpretations of messages from your past or what have you. If you can visualize that inner critic as an awful voice that isn't you, as a separate person who tells you lies, you'll be on your way to health.

I've even heard of people giving their inner critic's voice a different name, like "the old hag." Naming it puts it outside you and gives you leverage over it. You can start thinking, *I have to shut down the old hag* and *I'm not going to listen to the old hag.* You no longer identify with it because it's something coming from a source other than yourself. This habit will free you from its influence.

Finally, once you've recognized the voice and made it a separate entity who tells you lies, you can begin replacing those thoughts with better thoughts and better messages. Ones that build you up and lead to your success and happiness.

You've rehearsed those negative thoughts so much that they've built neural superhighways in your brain. But when you replace them with positive thoughts, you build new neural pathways, and *those* become the roads your thoughts run along.

Replace the old hag with something better, something that pulls for your good. That's the best way to defeat it. Build a voice that is your best friend. No matter what this critic told you, you actually do have the positive traits that the new friend is saying. And not only do you have those traits, but you're also growing into them moment by moment.

It takes a lot of effort to retrain your thinking. But you can do it, and it will stick. That's just the way the brain works. The brain always runs to what you believe. The brain looks for evidence in your environment that matches up with whatever you believe to be true about you. So make sure you believe things about yourself that lead to your total well-being.

I have struggled in my journey. I like to be playful and lighthearted, so it may surprise you to learn that I have had death threats made against me. People have made threats against my wife and children.

We had to move out of our home because it became unsafe. You don't go toe-to-toe against evil and not have evil come looking to take you down.

So when I say that your why is essential to keep you going, I know of what I speak.

Your why powers you through when you're tempted to quit. In this book we've seen several people say that sometimes quitting is a viable option, and I believe that's absolutely true. But I also appreciate the perspective of entrepreneur Jordan Schrandt: "Do. Not. Quit. Instead, learn to rest. Learn to surround yourself with wise and truthful counsel. Learn to block your time and keep a good schedule. Learn to have fun. Remember, the sun is still going to rise tomorrow, and the birds will sing, no matter what happens today. Nothing is worth losing your sanity over. So remember your why, and don't quit. Rest up, step back, gather your team, tackle the big things first ... and then keep walking."

It's the why behind what you are doing that gives you momentum. Yes, frustration matters. Yes, innovation is important. But your why is what gets you out of bed. Your why is what helps you have those difficult conversations about conflict. Your why is what helps you keep your team motivated. And your why is what helps you move past being not OK.

Because what you are fighting for is more important than how you are fighting. Your what will evolve. But your why is what energizes the whole pursuit of your impossible.

Do you know your why?

I'll end this chapter with a story from Pastor John Siebeling about when he was on the verge of changing direction in the days before things began to grow.

I remember sitting on the front row of our church in the hardest moment of our history. I didn't know whether I could go on or whether I even wanted to go on. And even though I'm a pastor, it doesn't necessarily mean I hear the audible voice of God on a daily basis. But on this day, when I was really feeling low, I sensed a very clear impression in my spirit. It was as if the Lord was letting me know He understood I didn't want to keep going. In the most loving, fatherly way, I felt Him telling me that if I decided not to continue, He would release me from the calling. He was giving me the freedom to choose.

I have to tell you, it was so powerful. But it absolutely scared me. Here was the freedom to quit that I thought I wanted, but when it was there, I immediately saw that I didn't want to stop. The idea that the Lord would release me from the calling gave me the perspective I needed. It instantly confirmed in me the conviction to keep going, because I didn't want the Lord to release me from something He'd called me to do.

Right now you have the freedom to quit as well. Maybe it's time. Maybe you need to pivot. You can go do beautiful things in another arena.

You may instead find that remembering the why behind the what is for you what Pastor John's releasing moment was for him. It may give you the clarity you need to see what to do.

DISCUSSION QUESTIONS

1. What is the why behind your what?
2. Are there circumstances where you have forgotten your why? If so, how do you reenergize yourself to be why focused?
3. If someone gave you the freedom to quit your endeavor, would that make a difference in your thinking? How does feeling that you're *not* allowed to quit play into feelings of burnout?

DEAR TWENTY-SIX-YEAR-OLD ME

For a while some friends and I have been doing a podcast called *Dear 26 Year Old Me*. In a style similar to this book, we invite leaders to be interviewed about what they've learned in business and life and wish they would've known when they were just starting out. The focus of the program is to give listeners the best advice and lessons business professionals learned so that, hopefully, listeners will be able to apply this wisdom to their own lives—perhaps at a younger age.

It's fitting, then, that we should have a chapter on what the amazing people we've interviewed for *Relentless Pursuit* would say to their twenty-six-year-old selves.

I'll start with something I'd say to my younger self.

Leaders have traditionally been challenged with the need to always present a perfect image. They are expected to be a display case or shop window and an example and to present an unrealistic level of achievement. If I were to say one thing to my twenty-six-year-old self, it would be this: people don't want perfection; they want authenticity.

It's OK not to be OK. People don't need your perceived perfection; they need the real you, warts and all, falling and getting back up again, apologizing and empathizing and walking forward.

How I wish I'd known that early on! It would've saved me a lot of unhappiness and that feeling of being false, which I'm sure I communicated to the members of my team. But we're all young and dotty at first, aren't we?

Now let's hear what my friends would say to their younger selves.

ANDREW BURTON

Here are the five things I would tell my younger self, if I could.

First, make sure you are very well funded in your endeavor. I would actually recommend that you be overfunded. You're much better off raising too much money to start your venture than too little. If you're overfunded and you do really well out of the gate, you could give some of it back. But if you're underfunded, you could run out of money and instantly be in a crisis.

At Thrifty we mandated that franchisees raise £100,000 ($120,000) to set up the business and have an additional £25,000 ($32,300) raised for when it didn't go to plan. We wanted them to be able to sleep at night. We wanted them to be able to pay their bills on time all the way through whilst they were building their business.

Second, surround yourself with great people. At Thrifty we had a wonderful board of directors and fantastic people in every position.

There's no way we could have done as well as we did without those people around us.

Third, don't tolerate underperforming people. Deal with them quickly. It really is true that one bad apple could spoil the whole thing for everybody.

Fourth, make it your goal to listen to people. You don't actually have all the answers. You don't have all the knowledge. You're not the white knight or the complete man or woman. Complaints from your staff aren't something to be ignored or squelched—they're a sign that something isn't working. The complaints might be off or wrong, for certain, but normally there's a kernel of truth in every criticism.

So listen to your staff. Listen to your customers. Listen to your shareholders. They may be angry, but they may also be telling you exactly what needs fixing in your organization. We're throwing away helpful correction when we don't listen to complaints. Also, you have to celebrate what you want to replicate. If you want to create a culture of listening to correction, it has to start with you. Sift what these people are saying so you can find what you need to learn from it, rather than constantly defending your position. Don't be afraid that people may not always like your ideas or your product. Just sit back and be brave enough to listen.

Finally, do the right thing always, even if it is not the financially expedient thing. This will reap dividends in the long run.

Whenever we talked with a potential new franchisee at Thrifty, we would say to the franchise prospect, "Here's a list of all our other franchisees. Go and speak to any one of them about us." We were confident that every one of them would say we were people of integrity. That comes from doing the right thing even when—or perhaps especially when—it's not in your best financial interests to do so. And when we eventually sold our business, our reputation for honesty and integrity played no small part in giving confidence to the buyers to proceed with the purchase.

You may not make as much money in the short term, but you will develop a reputation for dealing rightly with people, and you can't measure the value of that.

NATALIE GRANT

I would say, "Don't wait so long to be comfortable in your own skin."

It took me well into my thirties before I became super comfortable with who I was. I had to stop wanting to run somebody else's race, which I had wanted to do because that race looked so beautiful. I finally accepted that it was actually OK to run my own bumpy, pothole-filled race. My race was beautiful too because it was the race God carved out for me.

The second thing I would tell myself is "You actually are enough." I know that sounds like such a bumper sticker, but it's still true. And it's one thing to say it, but it's another thing to live it. It's another thing to actually find your identity in Christ. I think one of the biggest tricks of the Enemy is to disrupt people's identities and keep them from understanding that they are enough as they are. If he can disrupt a person's identity, he can disrupt everything.

I had to accept that I'm enough because of my identity in Christ and that I have an inheritance as a child of the King. I would tell my younger self that discovering your true identity in Christ is so much more important than the dream you're chasing. Chase your identity in Christ instead of chasing your dreams. When you do that, your dreams will be something far greater than you could ever imagine for yourself.

But this is a daily process. I still struggle to remember these things. I put up sticky notes everywhere to remind myself of what is true. And I surround myself with a community of like-minded people who build me up and whom I can build up in return. Whom you're running with is so important.

JEN JORDAN

I had my first baby when I was twenty-six. When I held him, I was so fulfilled. I thought, *This is it. This is my whole world, right here in my arms. This is all that matters.* We had another child soon after, and being their mom was the only thing I wanted.

But if I could speak to my twenty-six-year-old self, I would say, "Hey, it's wonderful that you're loving this time. Treasure it. But let me suggest to you that there's more. There's more for you beyond being a stay-at-home mom. Not that there's anything wrong with that, but opportunities are coming your way where you can literally save the lives of children around the world. The child in your arms is incredible, but what if you could affect children and families across the world? What you have is great, but start opening your mind to the idea that bigger things are coming."

My twenty-six-year-old self never would have believed she could have the impact I'm having now. I would want her to keep her eyes open for amazing days ahead.

KEVIN KIM

My twenty-six-year-old self had an immature view of the place of failure and challenges in life. When I was twenty-six, I looked at a failure or a challenge as an obstruction, as something standing in the way of me doing what I wanted or doing what God was calling me to do. I know better now, but I wish I'd learned this sooner.

I love this verse: "Our light affliction, which is but for a moment, worketh for us a far more exceeding and eternal weight of glory" (2 Cor. 4:17 KJV). What if our challenges and disappointments aren't working *against* us but are actually working *for* us? What if failures, challenges, and disappointments are our teammates? What if they are actually our employees and they're there to do a job? And what if their job is to help us grow, to help us learn, to refine us, to make us deeper and stronger, and to make eternal investments for us?

Silicon Valley is known for celebrating failure. They have mantras like "Fail fast, fail often" and "Move fast and break things." To companies like Facebook and Google, failure doesn't mean "game over"; it means "try again with experience."

What I wish I could tell twenty-six-year-old me is "Who you will become is because of your failures and disappointments. You'll actually be better because of them. You'll make better decisions. You'll be slower to panic. Practically speaking, failure will teach you to be a better decision-maker and problem solver."

Failures are like those afflictions 2 Corinthians talks about. They're only for a moment, and they're investing for you; they're achieving for you; they're producing eternal glory for you. Don't hate your failures or curse your challenges. Embrace failure and disappointment as mentors who will shape you and friends who have an important role.

I would also urge my younger self not to squander resources, the greatest of which is time. I would say, "Don't play video games. Don't binge on Netflix. Time is your most precious gift and resource."

I think having kids heightens your perception of how time works. Time seems to go by way faster now. I blink my eyes, and my daughter, whose birth I remember so clearly, is now in middle school.

I'm forty-one now, and my biggest regret is that I didn't use my time wisely when I was twenty-six. I wish I had read the Bible more. I wish I had prayed more. I wish I had learned another language. I wish I had spent more time perfecting the craft of leadership. I wish I had learned how to surf.

If I could go back and give advice to myself at twenty-six, I would tell myself not to squander my time.

DAVID KINNAMAN

When I was around twenty-six, I was doing more and more management at Barna Group. I remember going to George Barna and saying, "You know, I really want to have an impact on my generation, like you had on your generation. I don't want to be only a manager—I really want to be a leader." I wasn't disparaging management, but there were certain things I wanted to accomplish that a manager would never have permission to do.

If I had the chance to talk to my twenty-six-year-old self, I would say, "Just be patient. It will come. Don't push. Trust God's timing."

When I was that age, I had aspirations to write a book, to lead a business, and to do all these big things. That was good, you know? I think it was part of how God was preparing me for doing important things in the world and for having a broader place of leadership.

One thing I did do well was to explore multiple areas of the company. At that point I was doing all sorts of things at Barna that if I had been really focused on improving my résumé, I shouldn't have been doing. They seemed really off topic. I was dabbling in this and that. I was doing desktop publishing and media interviews. I was in management. I was hiring and firing people. I ran a call center. I wasn't concentrating on things that would be a clear benefit to my career as I saw it then. I felt confident in my role in the company, so I learned all those disparate skills.

But guess what? Every one of those things ended up serving me now that I'm CEO. It's amazing that I know about hiring and firing, about management, about working with media, about call centers, and even something about what presentations and publishing should look like. Without realizing it, I was being groomed for something bigger.

Somehow I'd like to communicate this idea to my twenty-six-year-old self. But maybe it's best that I didn't know! I probably would have messed it up if I'd been trying to reach the goal rather than messing around.

I was too impatient at that time, trying to get ahead, trying to do all the big things right away. But sometimes it takes time to get to the spot where you think you want to be. And then when you finally get there, you realize that all that character building and shaping of your soul have really mattered.

Because it turns out that being a good leader is not so much about choosing the right project or finding the right employee. It's really who you are as a person that matters most. Not just whether your strategy is sound, whether people can trust you, and whether they want to work with you. But who you are at your core.

APRIL POINTER

What would I say to myself when I was twenty-six? I would say, "Don't wait until your midlife crisis to find out who you are."

What is a midlife crisis but the thing that happens to people who reach the age of fortysomething and realize they don't know who they are? They don't know what matters to them. They don't know what they're good at—or what they could get good at. They don't know what they want. They don't know what they want to achieve.

All their lives up to this point, they've been just doing what seemed best to do next. Now they're realizing they've lived this long and they have no idea where they wanted to be by now. Perhaps they're seeing that they're no closer to the dreams they had when they were young. And they go into a panic. They don't know who they are or how they got here, and they go crazy. They think, *Well, better late than never. I'll just do it all now.* And they lose their minds. They get divorced and buy motorcycles and have plastic surgery in a frantic effort to make up for lost time.

I think that's such a tragedy and such a waste. Why not wake up and have that conversation with yourself when you're twenty-six … or younger?

If you spend time in your twenties diving into those questions in regards to your relationships and your jobs and your experiences and your travels and you collect that data and the answers to those questions, you'll be way ahead of everyone else.

If you do this, by the time you're thirty, you will have a really good sense of who you are, what you're good at, and what matters to you. You will have a powerful foundation for when you do finally hit midlife and beyond. You'll know what you want to do and be, and you'll be sitting there with (hopefully) forty work years left.

I hate to see people freak out in their midthirties or so. And if they do finally figure out what they want to be and do, it's great, but they've lost years that they could've used to pursue their real goals and passions.

No matter how old you are, though, it's not too late to sit down and ask yourself who you are and what matters to you. List your strengths and values. Point the rest of your life in the direction you really want to go.

Yes, if I could tell my twenty-six-year-old self one thing, it would be to collect that important data and answer those life questions while I'm in that window of time. Doing that in your twenties can get you to a good place of understanding what you want to draw from the world and what you want to contribute to the world. It will give you a much deeper sense of who you are, and you can apply that knowledge for decades to come.

Why not start a couple of decades earlier and live a life of purpose?

ERIN RODGERS

What I would tell myself as a twenty-six-year-old is this: "You have no idea what's about to happen."

What it all boils down to for me is that I could never have explained to myself what was coming. It would have been impossible for me to explain how much things were going to change and that so much of what I assumed my life would look like was wrong. It's so much better than I assumed it would be.

I would also say, "Erin, what you think is important today is not what's going to be important to you in ten years. So just keep an eye out for opportunities that are coming. Constantly reevaluate what you maybe never would've thought you'd find yourself doing, because there are going to be a lot of better opportunities that come your way. Nothing is going to look like a straight line. There are no straight paths to success. It's going to feel insane for a long time. But hang in there, because it's that insanity that drives you to your goals. Nobody likes to hear that, but it's true. The thing that makes you crazy may just lead to your bliss."

It's those seasons when nothing makes sense and when you're surrounded by question marks that can point you to where you didn't know you wanted to go. There was a time when I thought God wanted me to move from pharmaceutical sales to teaching high school in the inner city, but there was no clear direction from Him about it. I was in a season when I was really seeking the Lord. I was constantly in prayer and constantly talking to wise people around me. And everybody said, "I don't know. This doesn't feel clear for you one way or the other."

I got to the end of my rope. I remember yelling at the Lord one morning. I don't know whether it was audible or internal, but I was screaming, "I'm not doing this. I'm done. I cannot make this decision. I don't know what I'm supposed to do. You are going to have to pluck me out of this current job and drop me in the middle of the classroom, if that's what You want, because I am not doing this anymore."

A week later, I got a phone call saying I had been laid off.

I had to laugh. I had gotten my clear answer! It came after an insane time, but when it finally came, it was undeniable. I had asked God to take me out of the job if He wanted me to go teach, and that's exactly what He did. I walked out of the job and into that school. Even though, in the midst of it, it felt ridiculous to cut my pay by three-quarters and step into a brand-new career that I didn't even have a degree in.

How could I get my twenty-six-year-old self ready for that kind of craziness? It was super risky and scary and made no sense. But I decided I was going to be all in.

JORDAN SCHRANDT

As I write this, I was twenty-six only six years ago. That's the age I was when I started as an entrepreneur.

My best advice is to know yourself and constantly reflect on who you are and who you want to be. Self-improvement and self-awareness go hand in hand. Choose what you want your best self to be; then don't let others be naysayers or impose on you who they think you are.

Admit it if you've had a moral failure, but otherwise, haters are going to hate and feel justified in doing so. Ignore them—they're not your tribe.

Run for your dreams, love your family and take them with you, don't be afraid of what people may think ... and just be awesome!

JOHN SIEBELING

I think there's a level of brokenness that you have to get to before you will really rely on God's ability to do something in your life. So long as you think *You got this*, you may not really believe that you need God's help. But the good stuff doesn't come until you hit the point where you realize, *I can't do this.*

The thing you're doing may be something that God has actually called you to do, but you have to understand you can't do this in your own strength, and you sure can't sustain it without Him.

When someone has that moment, it can be pretty tough. That's when you can come alongside that person and say, "Hey, it's OK. We've all been there. You're going to get through it."

The other thing I would tell my twenty-six-year-old self is "Stay with it; stay with it; stay with it. Just because it seems to be touch and go doesn't mean you should stop."

Finally, I'd say, "Begin with the end in mind. How do you want to finish this?" I'm in my fifties as I write this, so I'm thinking a little bit differently than when we started the church and I was in my late twenties. The older I get, the more thankful I am that I didn't quit. I'm thankful that I kept my good reputation and fought for the things that were important in the early days. Because of that, I'm now enjoying the way things are going, and they're closer and closer to the picture I saw in my heart at the beginning.

DR. ROBI SONDEREGGER

I would tell my twenty-six-year-old self to put certain priorities, personal disciplines, and wealth principles into place much earlier. Rather than telling myself to buy a certain stock that would make me millions of dollars, I would be more insistent on telling myself to develop discipline—to put formulas in place for healthy living (and to exercise the discipline to stick to those formulas).

My twenty-six-year-old self was very ambitious and would go running after all sorts of opportunities. But I discovered over the years that whatever you chase tends to run from you. Learning the discipline of building rather than chasing would have helped my young self move beyond accomplishments and success and more toward making what matters. What matters is *meaning*.

I would tell myself to prioritize family over fortune. Invest in people, not just projects. Wealth is birthed out of discipline, not ambition. If you have the right meaning or purpose in place, you can prioritize what matters. By building a quality marriage and intentionally investing in the lives of sons and daughters, you amass the kind of treasure no moth can eat, no rust can destroy, and no thief can steal (see Matt. 6:19–20).

SIR BRIAN SOUTER

I actually was twenty-six years old when we started Stagecoach. The advice I would give would be to always be willing to delegate things to other people. I think the twenty-six-year-old is always a bit of a control freak and thinks he or she is the only person who can do it or the only person who can do it well.

I think I could have saved myself an awful lot of effort if I had realized that I can delegate a task to someone who will do it almost as well in some cases, or, if I'm being honest, much better than I could. I quickly worked out that the best way to do this was to surround myself with people much smarter than me, which I set about doing.

Sometimes you do have to do it all yourself. For one thing, you're the most passionate about it, and maybe you're broke and can't afford to pay someone else to do it. But I recommend that you delegate more things to more people more quickly. Definitely I would want to say to my younger self, "Let go, bring other people in, and delegate."

My father gave me a lot of really good advice. One thing he said was to keep your money turning. Take a quick turn on something and then move on to the next thing so you keep your money moving. He also said, regarding negotiations, not to be too greedy but to make sure you leave something in it for the next person. And he told me that if you buy something at the right price, selling it is easy.

PATRICK THOMPSON

I would tell my twenty-six-year-old self that I'm a more resilient person than I thought I was. I'm stronger than I thought. Perhaps I considered myself a wee bit fragile. But I'm not.

I'm also stronger when it comes to facing conflict than I thought I was. As a band we've worked through some serious stuff together. We've made some hefty decisions about who should be on the team and so forth. We've worked through various legal issues and deep conflict with one another too.

I really, really hate conflict. I am a nine (peacemaker) on the Enneagram. I hate conflict; I avoid it with everything in me. But you can't live on the road and be at peace with one another at all times. So I've worked through conflict and learned to meet it head on.

Really, I have to credit my wife for teaching me that. On more occasions than I would like to admit, I've wanted to brush conflict under the rug, but she's said, "No, you need to stand up for this. You need to actually tackle that head on. You can't let that situation unfold the way it's going to." That would've been my default solution ten years ago: just take a back seat and let others sort it out. What I would tell my younger self is that it's not so bad—and sometimes it's good—to face conflict and not avoid it.

The other thing I'd tell my younger self is about leadership. I wasn't thinking about any of this ten years ago, but now I know that people work most effectively when they feel respected. People thrive when they feel you're alongside them and when they feel as if they're part of the team.

That's something I still need to get better at. In our business there are five of us up on stage. We are very much the face of Rend Collective. People know us and want our autographs and such. We're the ones who sort of strut around and get the applause. But Rend Collective is made up of a lot more people who do a ton of work but who get zero credit publicly. It takes a particular brand of person to not really mind about that.

I have realized so many times that we need to praise and include and encourage and appreciate the folks who work alongside us off-stage. We have to help them capture a little piece of the vision and own it for themselves. Theirs is thankless work—believe me.

But if they know, at the end of the day, that someone in the audience came back to God because the person in the crew carried the instruments from the lorry or that someone in the audience went home and made things right with his or her parents in part because that team member made sandwiches for everyone or ran and got cough syrup at the chemist's, then it helps them. They're going to work more effectively and they're going to be happier, because they know that *God's work goes on because of them* and that they share equally in any victory.

In the final analysis, we're a team. We're a community. And that's true only whenever everybody is going toward the same goal. This sense of community may make it a wee bit easier when we're asked at the last minute to put on a surprise show. It doesn't cost those of us who are onstage a lot of extra time to do that, but it takes the crew an enormous amount of time and work. That's what gives them sleepless nights and aching backs.

But if they have the vision and know what it is that they're a part of and they feel as if they are involved in people being encouraged by the music and moved closer to God, they can do it.

That's what I'd tell my younger self about leadership. Everyone shares in the wins God brings about through the work we do.

What an incredible assemblage of wisdom, wouldn't you say? If all we did with this book was package that one chapter and distribute it, I think it could change the world.

I trust you have gleaned much from it and will return to it again and again. I know I will.

DISCUSSION QUESTIONS

1. What would you say to your twenty-six-year-old self?
2. If you're around that age or younger, what would you say to your younger self?
3. What evaluated learning would you add?

THINK DIFFERENTLY

I hope *Relentless Pursuit* has inspired you to be deliberate about your words, about yourself, about your life, about your business and your ministry, so that now you recognize the power you have to construct your future through your words. I hope you see that you hold the ability to create good in the world and to create a wholesome and moral leadership through what you say. I hope you see that you can direct so much of what is and what's possible through the power of your tongue. I hope you see that you can, with your words, create a great future for your family and a legacy that is worthwhile.

I hope this book has prompted you to look at frustration differently. I hope now you're willing to lean across that old, worn table and ask questions of frustration. I dearly hope that now you see frustration not as just a problem but as a friendly motivation to positively affect other people's lives. I hope you see frustration as showing you exactly what business or organization you might develop that could employ people and bring good to the world. I hope you now see frustration as a gift for your life.

I hope this book has inspired you to constantly innovate. Innovation is an invitation, and opportunity is an invitation to innovate. Innovation will be your vehicle. I've taken innovation everywhere, and you will too.

I hope this book has inspired you to keep on pursuing and building a tribe so that you can develop people. Because no vision can be reached, no ministry can flourish, and no business can be done alone. It is not good for man or woman to be alone (see Gen. 2:18). You need a tribe who resonates with your vibe.

I hope you have realized that it is OK not to be OK but that it's not OK to camp there. You have to progress through life. Move from the valley to the hilltop.

I hope this book has inspired you to remember the why behind the what. It's so important that you have purpose in everything you do and that you remember the vision and communicate people's place in fulfilling it.

Lastly, I hope this book has inspired you with the knowledge that there are many leaders who have walked the same trail that you are on, and they have seen it through to completion. They have finished the race. They've finished it well and strong. I hope *Relentless Pursuit* has inspired you with the understanding that you aren't alone.

I suppose that's the biggest thing I've realized through this endeavor: leaders need to stick together. We need the company of other leaders, just to encourage one another daily, to encourage other people's visions, to talk about our common burdens, and to be champions and supporters of many.

PERSEVERE OR PIVOT?

When I set out to put this book together, I wanted to create encouragement that would help people keep going in the middle stage of an endeavor. They've started well and with so much energy, but the realities of the marketplace or the social issue they're up against or their own inability to do everything well has caused a significant setback. And, if we're being honest, significant discouragement. So I wanted this book to put wind back in their sails.

Consequently, when I interviewed the many amazing contributors to this book, one of my standard questions was what they would say to someone who was in that situation, who had met with significant headwinds and was thinking of quitting the journey.

I expected them all to say, "Press on! Be encouraged! Remember why you're doing this!"—and several of them did say that. But perhaps the biggest surprise out of all this was that several of them said, "You know what? Sometimes it really is the best idea to quit."

When I heard that the first time, my eyebrows rose, and I thought it was such a wise response. It's not always smart to keep going, after all. There are conditions in which it makes more sense to make a shift rather than to continue in a direction that you realize may not be the right one. But when person after person in these interviews said words to the same effect, I started to realize that this was an unlooked-for theme that was emerging in the book. Rather than edit it out, I embraced it.

One effect this book may have had on you is that you may have realized that you need to pivot rather than persevere. I can't speak for your situation, but if you are in that middle phase and you've lost your joy and you've lost your purpose, I suppose the challenge to you right now is … What are you going to do about it? Are you going to keep on going, or is it time? You've heard through some of the contributors, some of my friends, that maybe it's time to call it a day. And I want you to leave this book saying, "That's OK."

It's OK to have got your project, company, or ministry so far and to pass the baton to someone else. Look what you've accomplished! Look what you've made that wouldn't be in the world if you hadn't raised your hand and given your best! But maybe your part in this endeavor is done now.

Maybe you're in a business that is just stealing all your joy. Maybe you realize that you're very good at one part of this but what the organization really needs is someone—or multiple someones—who can take it to places you never could. Maybe it's not tenable, and no matter how hard you work, the initiative just won't be successful.

At the beginning of this book, I told you about my friend Mick, who had been in law enforcement. He taught me that it is not raw experience (even thirty years of it) that counts but *evaluated* experience. So maybe you need to do some evaluating right now. Maybe you need to reflect on your situation and ask yourself, *What do I want to do with my life? Is this the right place for me to be? Is there a good reason to keep going here, or is it time to put my energy elsewhere?*

As the hugely successful businessman Sir Brian Souter said in chapter 2, sometimes it's best to cut and run. It doesn't mean anything bad if you lay it down and focus on something else. It doesn't mean you're a failure. It doesn't mean you're a quitter. It means you're evaluating your experiences as you have them and you're learning where best to invest your resources.

Maybe you know it's time to pivot but you've been ignoring that realization. Maybe you're just pushing it down. If so, maybe this is the moment when I'm speaking to you across the table, asking, "Is this you—this thing you're pursuing? Is this where you wish to be and spend your time, money, and energy? Is this leading to the outcome you've envisioned, and is there reason to believe it will get there? Or is it time to cut and run?"

FIGHT LIKE YOU

The story of David and Goliath is one of my favorites in the Bible. Did you know that David wasn't even supposed to be at the battlefield? He hadn't been invited. His brothers were there, and the king and his army were there, staring across the field of battle at the Philistine army. But David wasn't supposed to be there. His dad had sent him to take some bread to his brothers and some cheese to their commander and find out how things stood. I can see the soldiers saying, "Oy, cheese boy, have you got any gorgonzola?" And David says, "I'm all out of gorgonzola at the moment, but I've got some cheddar."

When David got to the battlefield and heard and saw what the situation was, his conclusion was different from everyone else's. David saw what everyone else saw, but he had a different perspective. Everyone was talking about how big Goliath was, how tall, how mighty, and how he was undefeated—and all of that was true. But David knew a different truth. He said, "Who is this ... Philistine that he should defy the armies of the living God?" (1 Sam. 17:26). David saw the same giant across the valley, but he thought differently about what to do about him. (Read 1 Samuel 17 for the whole story.)

Leaders have to think differently. Oh, for a generation of people who think differently about the world's problems! Who think differently about how we can combat them and about how to do it more effectively and more efficiently!

That also means thinking differently about where we are with our leadership and our organization and in the pursuit of our vision. Sometimes we're in the middle of a massive frustration, and we have to think differently about that too. Perhaps for you it's not right to keep pressing on so that you double down to get it done despite all odds. Sometimes you're called to other things, to different things, and that's OK.

But at other times or for other people, you have to push through those obstacles and pain points. Sometimes you have to keep going. You have to continue the relentless pursuit of your dreams. You need to push through so you can break out into that new territory, that new era, that new legacy that you are creating. Nothing great happens through ordinary acts. I'm a firm believer in the idea that there's always pain involved with excellence.

You may need to put down a responsibility that isn't really you. It's hard enough to carry all your responsibilities, but to do something and feel as if it's not really allowing you to be who you are … that's when it may be time to lay it down.

In the story of David and Goliath, one of the most poignant moments for me is when Saul learned that this boy, David, wanted to fight the giant. Saul brought David into his tent and put his own armor on this child. Can you imagine this young man being asked to fight in an old man's armor or according to an old man's way of doing things? Saul's armor was clunky, heavy, and so burdensome.

I think my favorite bit of the story is when David plucked up the courage to say, "This isn't me. I don't fight like this. I can't carry all this weight if I'm going to be me against this giant." So he took off the armor, and I imagine it felt so good for that burden to just fall off him. David realized—and this is something all of us need to learn—that the best way to fight is to fight like you really are (see vv. 38–39).

My friend, as you are reading this right now, consider, Are you carrying a burden that isn't letting you fight like you? Our world tries to create us. It tries to ram us into a certain way of thinking or being. It tries to say, "No, this is who you'll be. This is how you'll act. This is how you'll develop the business." Until, just like David in Saul's armor, you're weighed down and you no longer feel like you. Is that where you are right now? If so, then you need to listen to that small voice that's shouting out, "This is not me!"

You need permission to fight like you. Let me just suggest that may be why you've read this book. You've gone through your frustration. You've gone through innovation. You've built a tribe and all the rest, but you realize you're not fighting like you. Maybe you need someone to tell you it's OK to start being you.

My friend, that permission is fully granted. *You can be you.*

You know why? Because you are the greatest gift to your world. When you are healthy and you are fighting like you, you are precisely what your family needs. When you're free to be you, you are precisely what your business needs—you are precisely what this world needs. The world is desperate for people who are wholly secure in who they are and in what they have to give.

Whether or not you are facing setbacks and discouragement and whether you decide that you're on the right track or you decide to go in a new direction, you will be most effective when you've thrown off everyone else's armor and are unleashed to fight like you. Take the words and wisdom from all the people you've encountered in this book and add to them your unique view of the world. Whether your greatest project is the dream to end human slavery or the dream of restoring your family, you have the best chance of doing it when you've evaluated your experience and the experience of others and you're fighting like you.

BLESSING

Thank you so much for reading this book. Thank you for being part of this. I hope it has blessed you, challenged you, equipped you, and inspired you.

I started *Relentless Pursuit* with a story of me going to a place where I saw exploitation. I've seen it so many times. The fight against modern slavery has propelled me on my own journey from frustration to innovation, through building my tribe and remembering my why and being not OK but not camping there.

The middle of any great endeavor will be tough. Actually, if you're not hitting resistance and pushback, you might need to wonder whether you're doing it right. But when you remain committed to the goal you have, certain it's where you want to be, you will find success. You will make progress. I've been blessed to see so many lives changed and so many families restored. So much evil bested and so much oppression lifted.

You can do that as well. Bless you.

NOTES

INTRODUCTION

1. US Department of State, "2018 Trafficking in Persons Report," June 28, 2018, www.state.gov/reports/2018-trafficking-in-persons-report/.

CHAPTER 1

1. "Josephine Cochrane," Historical Inventors, Massachusetts Institute of Technology, accessed April 26, 2019, https://lemelson.mit.edu/resources /josephine-cochrane.
2. "Thomas Edison," History.com, last updated April 15, 2019, www.history.com /topics/inventions/thomas-edison.
3. Edgar Guest, "Sermons We See," YourDailyPoem.com, accessed April 26, 2019, www.yourdailypoem.com/listpoem.jsp?poem_id=2270.
4. Martin Luther King Jr., *Strength to Love* (Minneapolis, MN: Fortress, 2010), 93.

CHAPTER 2

1. Arthur Schopenhauer, quoted in Garson, "Research Is to See What Everybody Else Has Seen and Think What Nobody Has Thought," Quote Investigator, July 4, 2015, https://quoteinvestigator.com/2015/07/04/seen/.
2. John C. Maxwell, *Developing the Leader within You* (Nashville: Thomas Nelson, 1993), 103.
3. John Burroughs, BrainyQuote, accessed April 26, 2019, www.brainyquote.com /quotes/john_burroughs_120946.

4. Jessica Salter, "Airbnb: The Story behind the $1.3bn Room-Letting Website," Telegraph, September 7, 2012, www.telegraph.co.uk/technology/news /9525267/Airbnb-The-story-behind-the-1.3bn-room-letting-website.html.

CHAPTER 3

1. Winston S. Churchill, "The Gift of a Common Tongue" (speech, Harvard University, Cambridge, MA, September 6, 1943), International Churchill Society, accessed April 26, 2019, https://winstonchurchill.org/resources /speeches/1941-1945-war-leader/the-price-of-greatness-is-responsibility/.
2. Lawrence G. Calhoun and Richard G. Tedeschi, eds., *Handbook of Posttraumatic Growth: Research and Practice* (New York: Psychology Press, 2014).
3. Erin Roach, "Billy Graham, in TV Interview, Reflects: 'My Time Is Limited,'" Baptist Press, December 21, 2010, www.bpnews.net/34303/billy-graham-in -tv-interview-reflects-my-time-is-limited.
4. "Killed the Horse," Bible.org, accessed April 29, 2019, https://bible.org /illustration/killed-horse.

CHAPTER 4

1. Michael Jordan, quoted in Grant Freeland, "Talent Wins Games, Teamwork Wins Championships," *Forbes*, June 1, 2018, www.forbes.com/sites /grantfreeland/2018/06/01/talent-wins-games-teamwork-wins -championships/#78c166304c8f.
2. Derek Sivers, "How to Start a Movement," TED, February 2010, www.ted.com /talks/derek_sivers_how_to_start_a_movement?language=en#t-114254.

CHAPTER 5

1. Frank Newport, "2017 Update on Americans and Religion," Gallup, December 22, 2017, https://news.gallup.com/poll/224642/2017-update-americans -religion.aspx.
2. Barna Group, "The End of Absolutes: America's New Moral Code," Barna, May 25, 2016, www.barna.com/research/the-end-of-absolutes-americas-new-moral -code/.
3. Barna Group, "The End of Absolutes."

4. Steve Jobs, quoted in Carmine Gallo, "Steve Jobs: Get Rid of the Crappy Stuff," *Forbes*, May 16, 2011, www.forbes.com/sites/carminegallo/2011/05/16/steve -jobs-get-rid-of-the-crappy-stuff/#26cd826f7145.

CHAPTER 6

1. International Labour Organization, *Global Estimates of Modern Slavery: Forced Labour and Forced Marriage* (Geneva: International Labour Organization, 2017)," www.ilo.org/wcmsp5/groups/public/---dgreports/---dcomm /documents/publication/wcms_575479.pdf, 9–10.

CHAPTER 8

1. Simon Sinek, "How Great Leaders Inspire Action," TED, September 2009, www.ted.com/talks/simon_sinek_how_great_leaders_inspire_action ?language=en.

ABOUT THE CONTRIBUTORS

Andrew Burton

In the early 1990s Andrew and his brother acquired the UK master franchise of Thrifty Car Rental and built it from scratch into the UK's fifth-largest rental organization before successfully selling it in 2006. Since selling, Andrew has been involved in a wide range of commercial and charitable ventures, including a number of start-up businesses, either as an investor, director, or trustee.

Natalie Grant

Photo by Dominick Guillemot

Seven-time Grammy nominated Natalie Grant has become an iconic name in gospel music. She's been awarded the GMA Female Vocalist of the Year Award five times and has sold nearly four million albums. Natalie, however, uses her platform for more than just music. She is the cofounder of Hope for Justice and uses her voice to fight for those without a voice.

Jen Jordan

Growing up, Jen Jordan knew she wanted to be a doctor, but on her way to getting a degree, she realized that she didn't want the lifestyle associated with the health care industry. In her words, she "handed her dream over to God," and when a husband and then three children came into her life, she felt her decision was confirmed, and her role as a wife and mother took priority. "This was it. This is what I was made for," she says. Today she helps others become their own health advocates, and she feels certain that God prepared her for this role through her education and experience. "I feel like Young Living handed my dream back to me," she says.

Jen's experience with oils began around 2009, when her sister, April Pointer, who is also a Royal Crown Diamond, introduced her to Young Living. Jen relates that her initial response was not a positive one: "I thought she was crazy!" Jen started using oils two years later but then only as a "closet oiler," despite the fact that essential oils changed her life. She reluctantly taught her first class, thinking that the attendees would just go away after listening. But that didn't happen.

With a life motto of "Love God; love people," Jen has built her business around encouraging, empowering, and building up others. She explains that she is continuing a culture of positivity in the lives of the leaders she works with. Jen and her husband are inspired to continue that generosity with those they meet in everyday life.

Kevin Kim

Kevin Kim is the executive director of Crazy Love Ministries in San Francisco, cofounder of a faith-based technology organization called Basil Technologies, cofounder of a start-up called Common Coin, and an elder and pastor at We Are Church. He went to seminary near Philadelphia and received an MDiv (and a wife) from Biblical Theological Seminary. Kevin served at Menlo Church as director of innovation and worked alongside IDEO on a project called Catalyst. Kevin currently resides in San Francisco with his wife and three children: Karis, Ellie, and Isaiah.

David Kinnaman

Photo by Breanne Thompson Photography

David Kinnaman is the author of the bestselling books *Good Faith*, *You Lost Me*, and *unChristian*. He is president of Barna Group, a leading research and communications company that works with churches, nonprofits, and businesses ranging from film studios to financial services. Since 1995 David has directed interviews with nearly one million individuals and overseen hundreds of United States and global research studies. He and his wife live in California with their three children.

April Pointer

April Pointer found Young Living in 2009 and purchased a bottle of Thieves (now Thieves Vitality) for her husband's immune system. It worked and made them believers. Essential oils were the missing link in their home with her love of health, wellness, and natural living.

After two years of using oils, she looked at the income opportunity after enrolling a friend who desired to generate an income with Young Living. April decided it was time to take a shot. With the goal of getting her oils paid for each month, April began teaching monthly classes with her friend. "Teaming up had a major impact on our success," she says. Momentum set in, and it grew each month.

At Gold, April's husband, Jay, was laid off from his corporate job, and her Young Living income ended up being the plan B they never planned for. Jay found a niche in April's business while still pursuing his own goals. They went on to achieve Royal Crown Diamond in 2014.

The Pointers desire to build a culture of goodness, freedom, and legacy. "I want to build something that is going to outlive me," April says. They desire to make a difference and are passionate about establishing clean water wells, ending human trafficking, supporting disaster relief, and missions.

Erin Rodgers

Photo by Kristin Peddicord

As evidenced by her past careers as a pharmaceutical rep, high school math teacher, and photographer, Erin Rodgers is a keen multitasker determined to create a path to success for her family. When she first stumbled into the world of essential oils, she was a wife and mom simply trying to survive the first few years with little ones at home. In a period of mama desperation, she reached for essential oils to support her family's health—and she was stunned when they worked! She could see a new life for her family, and she didn't want to wait for it, so she jumped in.

Her simple effort to support her family's health and wellness grew into something bigger, and she knew she would never be satisfied if she kept quiet. When she saw other moms feeling frustrated, helpless, and confused, she started to tell her story.

Now years into their Young Living adventure, the family is more committed than ever to creating a legacy—to planting seeds without knowing whether they'll see them grow into a garden—and to sharing the opportunity of wellness and abundance with everyone around them.

Jordan Schrandt

Photo by Elise Abigail Photography

Jordan Schrandt was introduced to Young Living while working as a freelance writer for agricultural publications. Because of the purity of Young Living products, Jordan felt a need to leave a "toxic culture and chemical-laden society." Though her dream was writing and communications, she decided it was time to step away from writing about the harsh and toxic chemicals in food and products and instead focus on educating people about a lifestyle of overall wellness.

Today Jordan and her husband, Doug, run their Young Living business while also raising eight children. Jordan returned to her first love of writing and recently launched her own magazine—a place where she combines natural living with the publication world.

Jordan also enjoys playing the piano, running, homeschooling, and homesteading. She loves empowering women and sharing her faith with others. She says she's developed the most authentic friendships through Young Living, and she feels that her experiences with the people and products have added so much love and fullness to their lives and the lives of so many others.

John Siebeling

John Siebeling, along with his wife, Leslie, are the founders and lead pastors of The Life Church, a thriving, multicultural body of believers committed to serving people, developing leaders, and influencing generations. Though most of John's time and energy remain focused on pastoring, he regularly speaks with incredible ministries and organizations around the world. He is the host of The Life Church's television program and author of several books focused on helping people experience God's best and move forward in life. John and Leslie love living life to the full with their two children, Anna and Mark.

Dr. Robi Sonderegger

Dr. Robi Sonderegger is a devoted husband and father of five children. He is renowned for taking psychology from the front line to the home front and is a highly sought-after keynote speaker, having presented to over 1.5 million people in more than twenty-five countries. His teaching curriculums are used globally, with more than three hundred thousand having graduated from his programs.

Sir Brian Souter

Sir Brian Souter is cofounder and chairman of public transport company Stagecoach Group and received a knighthood in June 2011 for services to transport and the voluntary sector. Sir Brian is chairman of private investment vehicle Souter Investments and makes significant personal financial contributions to a variety of good causes through the Souter Charitable Trust.

Patrick Thompson

Photo by Mary-Caroline Russell

Patrick is the guitarist and a founding member of the worship band Rend Collective. Since 2007 he has been touring around the world leading worship and speaking on behalf of several Christian humanitarian organizations. When not on the road, he and his wife, Judith, live in Bangor, Northern Ireland.